30
Days to
Becoming
a Woman
of Prayer

Stormie Omartian

HARVEST HOUSE PUBLISHERS
EUGENE, OREGON

Cover by Garborg Design Works, Savage, Minnesota

Cover photo © Bigstock / Luna Vandoorne

Author photo © Michael Gomez Photography

THE POWER OF A PRAYING is a registered trademark of The Hawkins Children's LLC. Harvest House Publishers, Inc., is the exclusive licensee of the federally registered trademark THE POWER OF A PRAYING.

30 DAYS TO BECOMING A WOMAN OF PRAYER
Previously published as *The Power of a Praying® Life*
Copyright © 2010 by Stormie Omartian
Published by Harvest House Publishers
Eugene, Oregon 97402
www.harvesthousepublishers.com

ISBN 978-0-7369-5362-7

Library of Congress Cataloging-in-Publication Data

Omartian, Stormie.
    30 days to becoming a woman of prayer / Stormie Omartian.
        p. cm.
    Rev. ed. of: The power of a praying life. c2010.
    ISBN 978-0-7369-5362-7 (pbk.)
    ISBN 978-0-7369-5365-8 (eBook)
    1. Prayer–Christianity. I. Omartian, Stormie. Power of a praying life. II. Title. III. Title: Thirty days to becoming a woman of prayer.
    BV210.3.O54 2013
    248.3'2--dc23
                                                                    2012042175

Printed in the United States of America

13 14 15 16 17 18 19 20 / BP-NI / 10 9 8 7 6 5 4 3 2 1

For I know the thoughts that I think
toward you, says the LORD,
thoughts of peace and not of evil,
to give you a future and a hope.
Then you will call upon Me
and go and pray to Me,
and I will listen to you.
And you will seek Me and find Me,
when you search for Me with all your heart.

JEREMIAH 29:11-13

Contents

———

How Can I Make
My Life Work?

We are all trying to make our life work. And while we don't always know for sure when it's working, we definitely know when it's not.

When your life is working, that doesn't mean everything is perfect. It means you are in a place of peace with God, and you know without a doubt that you are in His hands and He will not desert you, leave you hanging off a cliff, or fail to be with you in challenging, difficult, or tough times. When your life is working, you have a deep and abiding certainty that things are going to work out for good in your future, no matter what is happening today. That means even when something goes wrong, you know you have access to a power that can make it right again. That power only comes from one source—God. And He has certain specifications for tapping into it. When we live according to those specifications—the way He wants us to live—our life works.

We all desire stability and consistency in our lives. It's not good enough to live by chance or luck. That is too unpredictable. We want to know we can count on having the ability to make right choices. We will never have the peace we desire if our life is not progressing well because we didn't have the wisdom to make good decisions. We want to be able to avoid doing anything stupid that will bring undesirable consequences. We want to have an ongoing awareness of our purpose and a sense of hope about our future. But where do we get that sense of purpose, hope, peace, wisdom, stability, and consistency? It comes from God. In order to achieve this in our lives, we must connect with God in a deep and powerful way. We cannot enjoy freedom, wholeness, or true success without this vital connection.

What Is True Success?

You were not created to live in bondage, brokenness, or failure after failure. You have been put here to live a life of God-given power, purpose, and accomplishment. God wants you to live in true freedom, true wholeness, and true success.

True freedom doesn't mean freedom to do whatever you want. It means being liberated by God from anything that keeps you from doing what *He* wants. It means being free to become more like the Lord every day so you can live the life He created you to live and become all He created you to be. It means getting free of the restrictions, fears, false beliefs, and negative emotions that keep you from moving in to all God has for you.

True wholeness means having all the brokenness of your life put back together in a lasting way that allows you to become a whole person. It doesn't mean you are perfect, but rather that the *Lord's perfection* can shine *in* you and work *through* you—not only for *your* benefit but also for the benefit of others. When anything in your life is broken, God can mend it and make it like new again. The presence of God's holiness can make you whole.

True success is the kind of success *God* has for you. His ways are different from the world's. Too often when people think of success, they envision being rich and famous. Or being at the top of whatever they do. But true success is not about wealth, fame, and worldly accomplishment. True success is knowing who you are in the Lord and never violating that. It's trusting that God has a good future for you, no matter how things *appear* at the moment. I've known too many wealthy, famous, and accomplished people who were miserable because they chased after a selfish dream of their own making. I have witnessed the emptiness of a life lived totally for oneself, and there is nothing truly successful about it. That doesn't mean wealth, fame, and accomplishments are all bad. If you are doing what God has called you to do and the Lord blesses you with those things, then they are good. And you can enjoy that kind of success as long as you are using part of what God gives you to help others.

True success doesn't mean you never have problems. It means whenever you go through a difficult time you have a deep sense that God is with you and will bring you *out* of it or *through* it successfully. It means you see the hand of God in your life, and you acknowledge His presence and His touch with a grateful heart.

True success means you have an understanding of the ways of God and the heart of God, and you find great pleasure in honoring Him by living according to His laws and His ways.

True success means living in close contact with God throughout each day and finding everything you need *in* the Lord and *from* the Lord. It's having a deep inner peace because you know God is on your side and always there for you. It's believing God is greater than anything you face and trusting that His power can positively affect every situation that threatens you. It's knowing in your soul that no matter what problem comes along, God has a solution, a way out, or a way through. It's unwavering faith that your prayers are heard by God and He will answer—in His way and His time. It's sensing the love of God in your life and being able to extend it to others in the manner He wants you to. It's trusting that God has the answer to every question you have, and so you stop obsessing over your questions and start trusting His answers.

True success is becoming who you were made to be—who you really are—and accepting that who you really are is *good*. This knowledge frees you from having to constantly compare yourself to others and always feeling that you come up short. It liberates you from the tyranny of images and lifestyles depicted on TV and in films, magazines, and books that can make you believe you are failing if you don't live up to them. Measuring your worth by those standards will turn your world upside down from what it is supposed to be. God has so much more for you than that.

True freedom, wholeness, and success can only be found when you are living a praying life. A praying life means staying close to God and praying about everything. It means listening to Him speak to your heart and into your life. It's walking so close to God that He can keep you away from danger and guide you where you need to go.

How Do I Get Close to God?

The way to get close to God and appropriate His power in your life is through prayer. Prayer is the means by which we communicate with God. It is the avenue through which we tell Him our fears, desires, and needs. Prayer is the way we quiet our soul and mind and let God speak to us. It is through prayer that we worship God—giving Him praise for who He is, and telling Him how utterly grateful we are for all He has done for us.

In prayer we intercede for the people and situations around us. In prayer we praise God for all He has done. And we thank Him in advance for all He *is* doing and *will* do for us in the future. When we pray, we can sense our relationship with God growing stronger, and we feel our love for Him and our dependency on Him deepening. The more we pray, the more we can see His hand of mercy, grace, and love guiding us daily. The more we pray, the more we realize that we cannot live without Him and His power.

The key here is coming to the realization that we cannot make life work on our own. We need the power of God. We must have the saving, redeeming, delivering, healing touch of the Lord because we need to be saved, redeemed, delivered, and healed. And good luck trying to do any of this on your own. Let me just save you the trouble of learning the hard way that luck isn't going to do it for you. Your life is not going to have love, peace, joy, fulfillment, power, healing, restoration, and transformation without the Lord. The reason I know this is true is because I have been there and done that. All my attempts to make life work on my own nearly killed me.

I had a childhood of abuse at the hands of a severely mentally ill mother. When I was able to get out on my own, I nearly overdosed on drugs and drank way too much alcohol. I became disillusioned by many wrong relationships and tried to cope with paralyzing fear, anxiety, and depression on a daily basis. Living a cover-up life of laughter on the outside and gut-wrenching emotional pain on the inside, never knowing when disaster would strike, being afraid to go to bed because of what horrible thing could happen in the night, and waking up with dread because I didn't think I could make it through another day—this is not a life that works, believe me! My life works now because of what God has done and *continues* to do in me and in my circumstances.

Does this mean my life is perfect and I never have problems? I wish! But the answer is no. I live in the same fallen world you do. I have the same enemy attacking me just as he does everyone else who doesn't go along with him. I've been close to death so many times I have lost track of the number. I have troubles like everyone else. But I have also been saved, rescued, set free, transformed, and made whole. What God has done for me, He will do for you. He is not a respecter of persons. He doesn't respect me any more than He does you. He has the same love, mercy, peace, grace, power, healing, hope, restoration, redemption, and true success in life for you too. It all happens as you get close to God in prayer.

Knowing What Your True Needs Are

You need to frequently be reminded of who God is and who you *are* and *can be* in Him.

You need to take charge of your thoughts and emotions, and seek to be delivered from anything that imprisons or restricts you so you can live in the freedom and wholeness God has for you.

You need to be deeply impressed with the knowledge of all Jesus accomplished on the cross so you are not continually wearing yourself out struggling to make something happen in your life that has already been accomplished.

You need to always follow the leading of the Holy Spirit so you can know God's will and be where you are supposed to be, doing what you are supposed to do.

You need to understand, recognize, and receive the gifts God has for you so you are not always striving for what He has already provided.

You need to know God's rules for life and be able to secure His help in fully obeying them.

You need to be free of guilt and able to maintain a heart of humility and repentance.

You need to receive God's forgiveness whenever you miss the mark He has for you and be able to extend forgiveness to others when they, too, miss the mark.

You need to have the fear of the Lord in your heart every day so you are in right relationship with Him, and then He will take away all tormenting fear from your life.

You need to be able to see and appreciate your body as the temple of the Holy Spirit so you can learn to care for it properly.

You need to experience God's love every day and be able to share it with the people He puts in your life.

You need to be free to wholeheartedly give to God and to others in the way He would have you to do.

You need to know God as your Healer and grow in faith that He can bring healing to you and to those for whom you pray.

You need to find breakthrough in your life through the godly discipline of fasting and prayer.

You need the ability to take control of your mind and not be tossed to and fro by lies of the enemy, who always tries to make you believe that his lies are the truth and God's truth is a lie.

You need to resist negative thoughts and emotions, and stop believing lies about yourself.

You need to speak words that bring life, and be able to seek the truth in all situations.

You need to move in the power of God and not live an overwhelming life of powerlessness in the face of difficulties.

You need to be rid of destructive relationships that not only don't add to your life but tear it down.

You need to recognize who your enemy is so that you can resist him and not assist him.

You need to be strong enough to turn away from all temptation to do anything that is not glorifying to God.

You need to learn to pray without ceasing so that you can enjoy emotional peace and contentment.

You need to surrender your life to God and live in a manner deemed holy by Him.

You need to grow in faith and not be tormented or restricted by doubt and instability.

You need to be able to unfailingly stand strong in all you know of God, no matter what is happening.

You need to be the kind of person who never gives up hope, regardless of how hopeless things seem, because your hope is in the Lord.

If you have a desire for any of these things I have mentioned above, then what you need is more of the Lord in your life. This book will help you to find that life-changing closeness with Him. It will steer you toward God and His Word and help you discover more of who He is. I pray that as you read it—perhaps one chapter a day, praying the prayer, implementing the suggestions, and reciting the biblical truths related to the subject at the end of each chapter—within 30 days you will sense that your relationship with the Lord has grown deeper and you will see that God has provided everything you need in order for your life to progress in a positive way. Don't feel you have to complete it in 30 days, however. I just know that a lot of you type A's like to do that. Speed is not what is important. Go at your own pace and spend as much time as you need on each chapter. I have placed some pages for personal notes at the end of the book. If in your reading you come across something God is nudging your heart about, you can use those pages to record your thoughts or prayers.

The following 30 chapters give you 30 ways to pray. I could write a book on each chapter because there is so much to know about every subject, but what I have given you here is still enough to be life changing. Don't allow the brevity of the chapter to minimize the importance of that subject to your life. If you grasp these 30 ways to pray for your life, you will be living a life of balance, purpose, freedom, wholeness, and true success. You will be living a praying life, a life dedicated to drawing close to God and communing with Him every day—a life that works.

Stormie Omartian

KNOW WHO
YOUR FATHER IS

———◆———

The whole point of living a praying life is to be close to God and to have a deep, solid, and unshakeable relationship with Him. A praying life allows you to be solidly aligned with the Lord by communing and communicating with Him throughout each day. This means not only knowing *about* God, but truly knowing *Him*—or at least as much as He can be known on this earth.

Knowing God starts with the *desire* to know Him and then *seeking* to know Him. From there it becomes a matter of wanting *more and more* of Him in your heart and in your life. The focus isn't on the praying. The focus is on the *One to whom you are praying*. Prayer is the means by which you deepen your relationship with God.

Knowing God fully takes more than a lifetime. It takes eternity. But God is a God who can be known here and now. In fact, He *wants* us to know Him. He wants us to be well acquainted with the many different aspects of who He is. Three distinct aspects of God, which are the foundation of knowing Him, are God the *Father*, Jesus the *Son*, and the *Holy Spirit*.

You may be thinking, *I already know that.* But I thought the same thing until I found out how easy it is to *think* we know and yet miss dimensions of knowing God that we forget, overlook, or fail to see. Or we focus on one aspect of knowing Him to the exclusion of the others. Because this so important, the first three chapters of this book are devoted to these three vital aspects of our one true God.

The Importance of Knowing God as Your Heavenly Father

Knowing God *as* your heavenly Father is different than simply being aware that God *is* your heavenly Father. One of the reasons people are bound up, broken, or experiencing a sense of failure about themselves and their lives is that they don't know God *as* their heavenly Father.

I know a man who felt he would never be able to fully understand who he really was because he had never known his father. That young man's father had been tragically absent from his life, and now—even well into adulthood—he struggled daily with the pain and loss of that relationship. An entire piece of his life was missing, and he felt that lack every day as he tried to reconcile his past with his present and future. He knew who his father was, but he had never known him *as* his father.

I believe the same is true for all of us with regard to our *heavenly* Father. We know God is our heavenly Father because the Bible tells us so. "I will be a Father to you, and you shall be My sons and daughters, says the LORD Almighty" (2 Corinthians 6:18). God desires that relationship with us. But do *you* know without a single doubt that God is a father who loves you, values you, cherishes you, watches out for you, provides for you, protects you, takes away your hurt, and restores you the way a good father should? Without this knowledge deep within your soul, you will struggle with how you think God sees you.

Children who *know* they are loved by their father act differently than those who *doubt* that they are loved or, even worse, *know* that their father doesn't care for them. The ones who *know* they are loved develop better and faster than those who *don't feel* loved. This is common knowledge. And it is just as important that we—as adults—understand the love our Father God has for *us*. In order to do that, we have to know Him better every day.

When you truly acknowledge God *as* your heavenly Father, you will have taken the most significant and foundational step toward finding the freedom, wholeness, and true success God has for you. When you come to know who your heavenly Father really is, then you can better understand who *you* really are. The good news is that you don't have to live in ignorance of who your heavenly Father is because He not only *can* be known but *wants* to be known by you.

When Jesus' disciples asked Him to teach them how to pray, He said, "Your Father knows the things you have need of before you ask Him. In this manner, therefore, pray, 'Our Father in heaven, hallowed be Your name'" (Matthew 6:8-9). He proceeded to give them what we call the Lord's Prayer. Jesus instructed the disciples to first establish their relationship with God as their heavenly Father. What that means for us is that we, too, need to begin our prayers by acknowledging God as *our* heavenly Father. If you want your life to work, begin each day by saying, "Thank You, heavenly Father, for this day."

The foundation of your entire relationship with God is that you are His son or daughter. That means you are dependent on Him for everything, and because He is your Father, you can trust Him to provide for you and protect you. After all, isn't that what a good father does?

Too often, however, people have a distorted image of God as a father because they had (or have) a bad or nonexistent relationship with their earthly father. If you felt unloved, abused, distant from, or abandoned by your earthly father, you may project those feelings onto God as well. But God is not distant or abusive. He loves you and wants you to love Him. He wants you to be with Him and to trust that He is with you. He is never too busy for you. He will always take care of you. He will never abandon you. He will not leave you or forsake you. He knows what you need (Matthew 6:8). He gives good things to His children who love Him, seek after Him, and ask of Him (Matthew 7:7).

Being a child of God means knowing you are part of a large family and you have a place with Him and that family for eternity. In the meantime, because you are His son or daughter, God will guide you, provide for you, protect you, and give you an important position in the family business.

Healing the Relationship with an Earthly Father

What was your relationship like with your earthly father? Can you see any way that you may have projected onto God some of the feelings you have had toward your father? This will be especially apparent if you did not—or *do* not—have a good relationship with your earthly father.

If your father was gone a lot or just never there for you, you may feel God won't be there for you when you need Him most, either. If your earthly father was emotionally detached, abusive, or stern, you may feel that your heavenly Father will be distant, unloving, or cold. The relationship you had with your earthly father can affect the relationship you have with your heavenly Father more than you realize if you don't take steps to keep that from happening.

If your earthly father was *far* from perfect, know that your Father God will never be *less* than perfect. If you were ever made to feel like a failure when you made a mistake, you may think God is always disappointed in you too. But your Father God is not like an earthly parent. He will never have expectations *of* you that are too high for you to meet. He does expect a great deal *for* you, however. He expects you to have the life of freedom, wholeness, and true success He has for you. All He asks *from* you is that you love, trust, and obey Him, and that you depend on Him for everything.

While you cannot control what your earthly father *did* or did *not* do in your life, you *can* control your response to that now. And it starts with forgiveness.

My mentally ill mother was very abusive when I was growing up. Even when her mental illness was later diagnosed, that knowledge still didn't take away the years of abuse I suffered at her hands. Once I became a believer, I learned that if I wanted to live in the freedom, wholeness, and true success God had for me, I had to forgive her. That didn't happen instantly. It happened a step at a time as I prayed for God to help me forgive her completely. And I eventually did.

In addition to that, I also had to forgive my dad.

I never consciously realized I had any unforgiveness toward my dad until my Christian counselor and mentor, Mary Anne, told me that God had revealed this to her. Even after I met with her about it, I didn't believe it. My dad never abused me, so I had a hard time receiving this. Mary Anne said, "Just ask the Holy Spirit to show you the truth."

When I was alone, I asked God to show me the truth about what Mary Anne had said. And I was totally shocked when He instantly revealed how much unforgiveness I had toward my dad for never rescuing me from my mother's insanity. He never unlocked the door to the closet my mother often put me in for hours on end as punishment. He never rescued me from my mother's physical, emotional, and mental abuse. Because my father had not come through for me as a child, I had a hard time trusting that my heavenly Father would come through for me as an adult.

When I confessed my unforgiveness toward my dad, I sobbed away a lifetime of uncried tears and resentment I had held within my heart. I discovered that only God's love and healing power can unearth things so deeply buried within us that we don't even realize they are there, and He can free us from them.

The freedom I felt after confessing my unforgiveness toward my father was pronounced. The most noticeable difference was that I sensed the love of God powerfully in my life as I had never felt it before. Forgiving my earthly father set me free to love him more, and to love and trust my heavenly Father more as well. After that, I saw my life open up to the love of God in ways I had previously not been able to do.

In order for you to have a solid foundation in the things of God that will determine where your life goes and what happens, and in order to have the freedom, wholeness, and true success you want, you have to forgive your earthly father for all that he *did* or did *not* do *to* you or *for* you. Your relationship with your earthly father may have been much better than mine or it may have been worse. Whatever it was, ask God to show you if there is anything, with regard to your relationship with your father, that needs to be forgiven or mended.

I am not saying that if your father was abusive or absent you have to go find him so you can talk to him in person. Some fathers will be receptive to that and some won't. Your decision about that is between you and God. Your father may not even be alive now. Whether he is living or not, forgive him for any way he failed, hurt, or disappointed you. The freedom of forgiveness I experienced toward my dad happened with just me alone with God. He can meet you where you are right now and do the same for you. If there are any bad feelings in your heart toward your father, bring those to God and ask Him to take all negative feelings and memories away, and heal you of any hurt associated with them.

Even if you think your earthly father couldn't have been a more perfect dad, ask God to show you if you are projecting any wrong or incomplete ideas about what a perfect father is onto the Lord. God may show you something about Himself that you didn't realize.

Your heavenly Father can heal you, mend your brokenness, and bring life to places in you that you thought were dead. The truth is, you can never experience the peace, freedom, restoration, wholeness, and true success God has for you without recognizing and acknowledging God as your heavenly Father. When you can truly accept God as the greatest father imaginable, it will positively affect every area of your life.

Find Out Who Your Heavenly Father Really Is

In the Bible, God is revealed by the many names He is called. I believe those names are there to help us better understand the many different aspects of God's character. They help us to know who He really is. We cannot move into the life God has for us without this knowledge.

The list of names below will help remind you of aspects about God's nature that you may have forgotten, overlooked, or perhaps have not known. God has revealed Himself in this manner because He wants you to know and trust Him in every way possible. In understanding Him by these names, and calling Him by these names, you invite Him to become that to you.

I have written this brief list of the names and attributes of God as a short prayer for you to say. It's a way for you to acknowledge God as the many aspects of who He is and help you to know Him better.

"Heavenly Father, You are my *Restorer.* You restore all that has been taken, destroyed, devoured, or lost from my life" (Psalm 23:3).

"Father God, You are my *Deliverer.* You set me free from anything that keeps me from the life You have for me" (Psalm 70:5).

"Heavenly Father, You are my *Redeemer.* You redeem all things in my life" (Isaiah 63:16).

✳ "Father God, You are my *Strength.* When I feel weakest, that's when You are strongest in me" (Isaiah 12:2).

✳ "Heavenly Father, You are my *Guide.* I acknowledge you in all I do, knowing that You are directing my steps" (Proverbs 3:6).

"Father God, You are my *Counselor.* You teach me all the right things to do" (Psalm 16:7).

"Heavenly Father, you are my *Peace.* When my life provides little peace, I can still find peace in You" (Ephesians 2:14).

"Father God, You are *Immanuel,* the God who is with me. You are always close and never distant. I am grateful that You never leave or forsake me" (Matthew 1:23).

"Heavenly Father, You are my *Strong Tower.* You are a covering of protection for me when I turn to You" (Proverbs 18:10).

"Father God, You are my *Hiding Place.* I can hide myself in You whenever I am afraid and facing more than I can handle" (Psalm 32:7).

"Heavenly Father, You are my *Wisdom*. When I need wisdom about anything, I can go to You, and You will give me all the understanding I need" (1 Corinthians 1:24).

✳ "Father God, you are my *Everlasting Father*. You are my Father forever, and not just until I can figure things out on my own" (Isaiah 9:6).

These dozen names are just a fraction of the many names of God, but they will provide a good foundation from which you can spend the rest of your life uncovering all of who God is. And you will love the process, because the more you know of God and the more you acknowledge Him in your life, the closer you will grow to Him.

God is your heavenly Father, who will guide, protect, and counsel you. He will deliver, restore, and redeem you. He will give you strength, peace, and wisdom. He will be with you always, so you can run to Him whenever you need a place to hide. "Our help is in the name of the LORD, who made heaven and earth" (Psalm 124:8).

Knowing God as your heavenly Father is the beginning of freedom, wholeness, and true success in life.

✣ PRAYER POWER ✣

Heavenly Father, I thank You that You have given me the right to become Your child (John 1:12). I am privileged and glad to receive all You have promised Your children. Help me to live in Your love and comprehend the depth of Your care and concern for me. Take away any barrier that keeps me from fully understanding what it means to trust You as my heavenly Father. Help me to take on a family resemblance, so that I have Your eyes, Your heart, and Your mind.

Lord, show me any way in which I need to forgive my earthly father. Heal anything in my heart that has caused me to see You through his failings. Forgive me if I have judged Your perfection by his imperfections. Show me what I need to see, and help me to completely forgive.

Thank You, Father God, that when I need hope, You are my *Hope* (Psalm 71:5). When I am weak, You are my *Strength* (Isaiah 12:2). When I am weary, You are my *Resting Place* (Jeremiah 50:6). When I need freedom, You are my *Deliverer* (Psalm 70:5). When I want guidance, You are my *Counselor* (Psalm 16:7). When I need healing, You are my *Healer* (Malachi 4:2). When I seek protection, You are my *Shield* (Psalm 33:20). When I am going through a difficult time, You are my *Stronghold in the Day of Trouble* (Nahum 1:7). Thank You for being my heavenly Father and the answer to my every need.

In Jesus' name I pray.

✣ WORD POWER ✣

When my father and my mother forsake
me, then the LORD will take care of me.
PSALM 27:10

As many as received Him, to them He gave
the right to become children of God, to
those who believe in His name.
JOHN 1:12

Look at the birds of the air, for they
neither sow nor reap nor gather into barns;
yet your heavenly Father feeds them.
Are you not of more value than they?
MATTHEW 6:26

When you pray, go into your room, and
when you have shut your door, pray to your

Father who is in the secret place; and your
Father who sees in secret will reward you openly.

MATTHEW 6:6

Behold what manner of love the
Father has bestowed on us,
that we should be called children of God!

1 JOHN 3:1

→ 2 ←

RECEIVE ALL THAT JESUS DIED FOR YOU TO HAVE

------◆◦×◦◆------

Without Jesus we are dead.

This is true in so many ways, because without Jesus we are separated from God. We need the resurrection life of Jesus *in* us so that we can be right with God and raised up to be with Him when we die.

However, Jesus not only gives us life for eternity—which is reason enough to receive Him—He also gives us more life in *this* life, for He resurrects the dead areas of our earthly lives in countless ways as well.

In my twenties, after I had finished my third year of college at UCLA and had returned from a tour of the United States with a well-known singing group, I started working as a singer/dancer/actress on musical-variety television shows popular at that time. It was through the people I met on these television shows that I got into alcohol and drugs. Neither I nor the people I worked with ever used drugs or drank while we were working. We were all too professional to do anything irresponsible like that. These jobs were coveted, and no one would jeopardize them for something so stupid. But at private parties and social events, alcohol and drugs were always plentiful. And not for sale, I might add. At least I never paid a penny for anything I indulged in. However, I found that drugs and alcohol provided only a *temporary* relief from the emotional misery I experienced every day of my life. I needed something permanent.

I wanted to be close to God because I figured He was the only one with the power to lift me out of the pit I was living in—or I should say *dying* in. So I tried every religion I could find except the Christian faith. The Christianity I had known—mostly through my mother—seemed somewhere between dead and a little crazy to me. While I thought the Christian thing was a really nice idea, I didn't see any power in it. Plus, I believed I would have to suspend all intellect in order to believe what Christians did. And the few times I went to church in my life I didn't feel any closer to God, and I didn't see anything change in me or my life. So Christianity was a nonissue to me.

In my search for God—and a way out of feelings of rejection, hurt, sadness, fear, depression, anxiety, and suicidal thoughts—I went full speed into one Eastern religion after another. In each one I found their god to be cold and distant. Unless, of course, you could *do* the things that religion's literature and leaders suggested in order to bring yourself *closer* to god. These religious to-do lists were either impossible or they just simply never worked. At least they didn't work for me. With each disappointment, I became more despairing of ever finding any solace in God.

I went deep into the occult as well. Too deep. That experience turned out to be stranger than any of the others. I was certainly having some kind of spiritual experience, but it was scaring me to death—literally. Looking back, I now recognize that the spiritual beings I was communicating with were definitely not of the Lord.

Finally, I got to the end of my rope and myself, and I contemplated suicide as the only way out of my pain. I had persistent suicidal thoughts. It was not that I wanted to die; it was just that I didn't want to live the way I was living. And I had found no way I could change myself or my circumstances. I felt I had tried everything I knew to find a way out of my misery, and nothing had worked.

At that time a Christian friend and coworker, Terry, invited me to meet her pastor. I went because I saw a quality in her I really admired.

She had something that made her life work, and I was attracted to whatever it was. To make a not-too-long story extremely short, Pastor Jack Hayford led me to receive Jesus. I never dreamed I would be doing such a crazy thing. But as it turned out, it was the best decision I ever made.

Right away things began to change. I felt hope for the first time in my life. Hope for a future. Hope for a lifelong purpose. Hope for freedom from the pain, depression, fear, and anxiety I had begun to believe was the way my life would always be. I discovered that while there was no way *I* could change myself and my circumstances, *God* could change everything. That's because I now had a relationship with Him through Jesus, His Son, who had paid the price for my freedom. Now, because I had chosen to have humble faith in Jesus, I had secured the avenue through which God's blessings could flow. But it was just the beginning of learning about all that Jesus did for me.

Receiving Jesus Is Just the Beginning

It's not enough to initially receive Jesus; you must also be daily mindful of *all* He did for you and receive that too.

Accepting Jesus as God's Son and your Savior gives you eternal salvation. When you die you will spend eternity with the Lord. That would be amazing enough if it were all He did, but He accomplished so much more. You need to have a clear understanding of the *full extent* of what Jesus accomplished on the cross and, as a result, what He has done for *you*. You must truly comprehend the many ways He has saved you. For example, you may know He has saved you from death and hell, but do you know and believe with all your heart that He has also saved you from infirmity, torment, depression, hopelessness, anxiety, and fear?

What Jesus has saved you *for* is to be with God forever and serve His purposes in all you do. What Jesus has saved you *from* are the consequences of living apart from God and His ways.

The Bible refers to Jesus as one "who gave Himself for us, that He might redeem us from every lawless deed and purify for Himself His own special people, zealous for *good works*" (Titus 2:14, emphasis added). He is purifying you as one of His special children in order for you to do good things for Him. The knowledge and sense that He loves you that much will make you eager to do what pleases Him.

Because of Jesus in You

It's vitally important that you understand all you really have in Jesus, because if you don't you will not be able to fully receive it. When life's circumstances challenge you, or the enemy tries to destroy you with his lies, you must know what authority you have in Jesus' name.

Below is a list of some of the things you have been given, because of what Jesus accomplished.

Because of Jesus, You Can Be Completely Free of Guilt

Guilt is something we all have, whether we feel guilty about the things we know we have done wrong or regret over what we feel we *should* have done better. Our shoulders were not built to carry guilt. It weighs us down and breaks us.

Most of us have a longing to "do over" some things in our life. My own list is long. We think, *If only I would have done this.* Or, *If I hadn't done this, then that wouldn't have happened.* Unchecked, the guilt we feel about the things we regret will destroy us. And until someone comes up with a time machine that works, we are not able to do anything to change all that has happened. We can refuse to think about it, but it will surface at some point in some manner anyway. And it will make us sick, miserable, angry, or depressed. However, when we receive Jesus, we are cleansed completely from our past. That means every mistake or violation of God's rules, ways, or laws is completely forgiven. The slate is wiped clean.

Again, you may be thinking, *I already know all this.* But you need to be convinced without a doubt that this is true, especially when the enemy tries to fill you with condemnation about things that have happened in your past.

The Bible says, "There is therefore now no condemnation to those who are in Christ Jesus, who do not walk according to the flesh, but according to the Spirit" (Romans 8:1). Notice it says, "*No* condemnation." That means none! It doesn't say, "Not very much condemnation." Nor does it say, "If you are in Christ Jesus, the condemnation you will feel is quite minimal." It says, "*No* condemnation."

When you receive Jesus, He takes away the condemnation of all your sins and mistakes of the past, and you are free from all that guilt. If you continue to feel guilt for the same things after that, you are not receiving all Jesus died for you to have.

If you have received the Lord and are still feeling guilty about the past, bring that to God and say, "Lord, I still feel tremendous guilt over what happened in the past. Please help me to live in Your full forgiveness and be able to forgive myself. Take away these feelings of guilt." God hears that prayer and will lift that guilt from you because Jesus already paid the price for that to happen.

If we do something wrong *after* we receive Jesus, He gives us a way out of that condemnation through *confession* of the wrong deed and through *repentance.* Repentance means we decide to turn away from wrongdoing and never do it again. It is important to know that the enemy will always make us feel *condemnation* about our wrongdoing. The Lord, on the other hand, will cause us to feel *convicted.* There is a big difference between the two. *Condemnation* leads to paralysis and death. *Conviction* leads to *repentance, confession, forgiveness,* and *life.*

Too often we continue to live with condemnation—which sucks the life out of us—and we must not allow it to do so. We must recognize that condemnation is one of the ways the enemy tries to separate us from God. The barrier of separation is not from God, however. We put it up ourselves. When we feel guilty about something, we hide from God. We don't want to face Him, so we don't pray as much or as effectively. The only way to stop that and clear the slate is by confession and repentance.

Because of Jesus, You Have the Holy Spirit of God Dwelling in You

When you receive Jesus, He gives the Holy Spirit to dwell in you. The power of God flows through the Holy Spirit, and now you have access to that power because He resides in you. (More about that in chapter 3, "Welcome the Holy Spirit's Presence.")

Because of Jesus, You Are Guaranteed Eternal Life with Him

When Jesus died and rose from the dead, He broke the power of death over you. When you receive Him, you also receive His resurrection life in you. "This is the will of Him who sent Me, that everyone who sees the Son and believes in Him may have everlasting life; and I will raise him up at the last day" (John 6:40). God promises to raise you up when you die, and the Holy Spirit living in you is the guarantee that He will keep His promise.

In addition to that, you also have access to His resurrection power whenever and however you face death each day—in your relationships, your health, your finances, your work, your dreams, or your abilities. Not only can God resurrect your dead body, but He can resurrect any dead area of your life as well. He is the only one who can give you life *before* death as well as after.

Because of Jesus, You Inherit What He Inherits

When you receive Jesus, you become a son or daughter of God. "If children, then heirs—heirs of God and joint heirs with Christ, if indeed we suffer with Him, that we may also be glorified together" (Romans 8:17). Being a joint heir with Christ means that whatever the Father has given His Son, He will also give to you.

Because of Jesus, You Can Now See into the Realm of God

We cannot see anything from God's perspective without receiving Jesus. We may believe with all of our heart that we are enlightened, but without accepting Jesus and receiving the Holy Spirit of God, we are spiritually blind. Once we have the Holy Spirit within us, we are now able to have godly discernment. Jesus said, "Most assuredly, I say to you, unless one is born again, he cannot see the kingdom of God" (John 3:3). All the intellect in the world will not allow you to see God and His kingdom.

Because of Jesus, You Can Rise Above Your Limitations

Jesus enables you to do what you could not do without Him. Jesus said, "He who abides in Me, and I in him, bears much fruit; for without Me you can do nothing" (John 15:5). He doesn't just help you to barely survive. He enables you to be liberated from the things that hold you back from all He has for you.

Because of Jesus, You Have Hope for Healing

Jesus is your Healer. He would not have come as your Healer if He didn't know you would need to be healed. This is such an important aspect of what Jesus does that I have devoted an entire chapter to it later in the book. (More about this in chapter 21, "Trust in Your Healer.")

Because of Jesus, You Can Enjoy Greater Abundance in Your Life

Jesus said, "I have come that they may have life, and that they may have it more abundantly" (John 10:10). Again, having abundance doesn't mean we will be rich, famous, and accomplished. It means He will give us more than we need.

Because of Jesus, You Have Become New

We all need a second chance—a new beginning. To be able to let the past go and become a new person is a miraculous gift. "If anyone is in Christ, he is a new creation; old things have passed away; behold, all things have become new" (2 Corinthians 5:17). When you receive Jesus, you are destined to become more like Him (Romans 8:29).

How Do I Know for Sure that I Have Received Jesus?

Your relationship with God is the very foundation upon which you build a life of freedom, wholeness, and true success. It begins when you receive Jesus and your relationship with God is firmly established. Peter said of Jesus, "Nor is there salvation in any other, *for there is no other name under heaven given among men by which we must be saved*" (Acts 4:12, emphasis added).

Jesus gives us salvation because we have faith in Him, not because of the good things we have done (Romans 9:31-32). He died for us because we are *sinful,* not because we are *perfect.* So we can come to Him the way we are. He wants us to come humbly to Him, knowing He did it all and we did nothing to deserve it. For it is "by grace you have been saved through faith, and that not of yourselves; it is the gift of God" (Ephesians 2:8).

When you receive Jesus, it is because God the Father is drawing you to Himself. Jesus said, "No one can come to Me unless the Father who sent Me draws him; and I will raise him up at the last day" (John 6:44). Receiving Jesus doesn't just happen by chance on a good day. It is not an accident.

If you want to receive Jesus, take these four simple steps:

1. *Believe that Jesus is who He said He is.* Jesus said, "I am the way, the truth, and the life. No one comes to the Father except through Me" (John 14:6). Say, *"Jesus, I believe You are the Son of God, as You say You are."*

2. *Declare that Jesus died on the cross and was resurrected from the dead.* "If you confess with your mouth the Lord Jesus and believe in your heart that God has raised Him from the dead, you will be saved" (Romans 10:9). Say, *"Jesus, I believe You laid down Your life on the cross and were resurrected from the dead to live forever so that I can have eternal life with You."*

3. *Confess and repent of your sins and failings.* "If we say that we have no sin, we deceive ourselves, and the truth is not in us. If we confess our sins, He is faithful and just to forgive us our sins and to cleanse us from all unrighteousness" (1 John 1:8-9). Repentance means turning away from sin and signifying that your intention is not to go back to it again. "Repent therefore and be converted, that your sins may be blotted out, so that times of refreshing may come from the presence of the Lord" (Acts 3:19). Say, *"Lord, I confess my sins and failings and I repent of them. I ask You to help me live Your way now so that I can become all You created me to be."*

4. *Ask Jesus to live in you and fill you with His Holy Spirit, and thank Him that you are now God's child.* "He who acknowledges the Son has

the Father also" (1 John 2:23). Say, *"Jesus, I ask You to come into my heart and fill me with Your Holy Spirit so that I can become all You created me to be. Thank You for forgiving me, securing my position as a child of God, and giving me eternal life with You and a better life now."*

If you said this prayer from your heart for the first time, indicating You are receiving Jesus, you are now adopted into the family of God. You have been forgiven; you are free from death, both now and eternally; and you have a secure future with the Lord. Write the date in your Bible so you can always remember it. It is the most important decision you will ever make.

Jesus accomplished so much for us, but too often we act as though He didn't. We live as if we have no hope, as though He is not the Healer or doesn't do miracles anymore, as if we are not made new and cannot ever have abundance of life in any form. We let ourselves become weighed down with guilt, afraid of death and living powerless lives all because we don't trust that we are truly a child of God and that we have the Spirit of God living in us. Don't let this happen to you. No matter what is going on in your life, remember that salvation is not only something Jesus did *for* you, it is also Jesus living *in* you. Therefore, you have whatever you need in order to face the past, present, and future of your life.

❖ PRAYER POWER ❖

Lord Jesus, I know You came "to seek and to save that which was lost" (Luke 19:10). Thank You that You saw my lost condition and have saved me for Yourself and Your purposes. Thank You that because You died for me, I have eternal life and Your blood cleanses me from all sin (1 John 1:7). Now I can live free of guilt and condemnation. I believe "there is no other name under heaven" by which I could ever be saved (Acts 4:12).

Thank You, Jesus, that I am a joint heir with You of all our

Father God's blessings. Thank You for reconciling me to Yourself (2 Corinthians 5:18). Thank You that I have the Holy Spirit within me and am no longer controlled by my flesh. Thank You that I have access to a life of hope, healing, power, love, freedom, fulfillment, and purpose.

Help me to understand all that You accomplished on the cross. Enable me to live like the new creation You have made me to be. Help me to see my life from Your perspective. Teach me how to receive all that You died to give me. Now, whatever I do in word or deed, help me to do all in Your name, Lord Jesus, giving thanks to God the Father through You (Colossians 3:17).

In Your name I pray.

⤙ WORD POWER ⤚

I am the resurrection and the life. He who believes
in Me, though he may die, he shall live. And
whoever lives and believes in Me shall never die.

JOHN 11:25-26

Behold, I stand at the door and knock. If anyone
hears My voice and opens the door, I will come
in to him and dine with him, and he with Me.

REVELATION 3:20

We have seen and testify that the Father has
sent the Son as Savior of the world. Whoever
confesses that Jesus is the Son of God, God
abides in him, and he in God.

1 JOHN 4:14-15

If Christ is in you, the body is dead because of sin,
but the Spirit is life because of righteousness.

ROMANS 8:10

I go to prepare a place for you. And if I go and prepare
a place for you, I will come again and receive you
to Myself; that where I am, there you may be also.

JOHN 14:2-3

WELCOME THE HOLY SPIRIT'S PRESENCE

As long as I live, I will never understand how anyone can find peace, hope, and fulfillment without Jesus and His gift of the Holy Spirit. Personally, I could not live without the presence of the Holy Spirit in my life. Nor would I want to even try. I did that for years, and I still remember the emptiness, pain, failure, and torment of dying a little each day.

So many wonderful gifts come with receiving Jesus, but the gift of the Holy Spirit is more precious than any other. I can see why the only unpardonable sin is blasphemy against the Holy Spirit. Only someone who is hopelessly evil would ever do such a thing. Those who truly know Him would never reject Him. Those who reject Him don't really know Him.

In order for you to have freedom, wholeness, and true success in life, you must be empowered by the Holy Spirit. Those qualities of life cannot be obtained without Him.

What Having the Holy Spirit Means for You

The Holy Spirit dwells in every believer. We receive Jesus because we have been drawn to Him by the Holy Spirit. The Holy Spirit then opens our eyes so that we are able to see the error of our ways and our need for repentance. When you open your heart to Jesus, you are filled with the Holy Spirit. From then on, you are on a wonderful adventure of discovering who He is and all He does in your life, and what having the Holy Spirit means for you. You are never the same again. There is a flow of the Holy Spirit within you, and you have to go with the flow.

Having the Holy Spirit Means You Belong to God

The whole goal of living a praying life is to be close to God and enjoy an ever-deepening relationship with Him. Receiving Jesus and being filled with the Holy Spirit is the means by which a close connection to God happens. The Holy Spirit in you is the guarantee that you belong to God. "You are not in the flesh but in the Spirit, if indeed the Spirit of God dwells in you. Now if anyone does not have the Spirit of Christ, he is not His" (Romans 8:9).

Having the Holy Spirit Means You Can Be Transformed

The Bible says, "Now the Lord is the Spirit; and where the Spirit of the Lord is, there is liberty" (2 Corinthians 3:17). We are set free in the Holy Spirit's presence. This is extremely important to remember. The freedom we find in the presence of the Holy Spirit doesn't mean freedom to do whatever we want. It is freedom to do whatever *God* wants so we can become all He created us to be. "We all, with unveiled face, beholding as in a mirror the glory of the Lord, are being transformed into the same image from glory to glory, just as by the Spirit of the Lord" (2 Corinthians 3:18). Transformation is found in the presence of God by the power of the Holy Spirit.

Having the Holy Spirit Means You Don't Have to Walk in the Flesh

If Christ is in you, then the Holy Spirit is in you as well, and that means you do not have to live in the flesh anymore. "If you live according to the flesh you will die; but if by the Spirit you put to death the deeds of the body, you will live" (Romans 8:13). This is about as clear as it gets. If we live according to our flesh—always doing what *we* want—we will destroy ourselves. Maybe not right away. Perhaps not today. But eventually, and possibly soon. But if we are Spirit led, we are able to put to death our desire to please the flesh every moment. Then we can live God's way and our life will work.

Being led by the Spirit doesn't only mean obeying specific commands of God but also being sensitive to the quiet promptings of the Holy Spirit at all times. It is having a sense from Him about what to do and when to do it, and knowing what *not* to do.

Having the Holy Spirit Means You Will Be with Jesus When You Die

The greatest news is that the Holy Spirit in you, who raised Jesus from the dead, will raise you from the dead too. "If the Spirit of Him who raised Jesus from the dead dwells in you, He who raised Christ from the dead will also give life to your mortal bodies through His Spirit who dwells in you" (Romans 8:11).

When I first became a believer, I worried that God might overlook me when I died. *How will He remember me?* But now I realize that the Holy Spirit in me will lead my spirit directly to God. It's a sure thing. The same is true for you too. He will not leave you or forsake you, for you are tied forever to Him. The Holy Spirit is a giant deposit in our soul that says we were bought and paid for, and our full redemption will happen when we go to be with the Lord. Until that time, the Holy Spirit in you gives you a sense of eternity every day.

Having the Holy Spirit Means You Can Be Led by God

Your thoughts, actions, and words can be led by the Holy Spirit, and this is another indication that you are God's child. "As many as are *led by the Spirit of God,* these are sons of God" (Romans 8:14, emphasis added). The Greek word for "led" here can also mean "*continually* being led." That means we can be prompted by the Holy Spirit throughout every day. The Bible also says to "be filled with the Spirit" (Ephesians 5:18). This passage also implies that we are to be "continually filled."

Having the Holy Spirit Means You Always Have Help and Hope

The Holy Spirit helps us in all things. "The Helper, the Holy Spirit, whom the Father will send in My name, He will teach you all things, and bring to your remembrance all things that I said to you" (John 14:26). The Holy Spirit fills us with hope and peace (Romans 15:13).

Having the Holy Spirit Means You Can Pray More Effectively

The Holy Spirit helps us to pray in power. "The Spirit also helps in our weaknesses. For we do not know what we should pray for as we ought, but the Spirit Himself makes intercession for us with groanings which cannot be uttered" (Romans 8:26). The Holy Spirit guides our prayers so that they are aligned with the will of God, and that makes them far more powerful and effective.

Having the Holy Spirit Means You Can Move in the Power of God

Because of the Holy Spirit within us, we have access to the power of God. We must never ignore that fact. We don't ever want to have "a form of godliness," but deny "its power" (2 Timothy 3:5). When we deny God's power, we shut off the full extent of His work in our lives. We limit what He can do *in* us and *through* us. Without His power, we cannot rise above our own limitations or withstand all that comes against us.

Having the Holy Spirit Means You Have Access to God's Wisdom and Truth

We can't do what we need to do without the wisdom of God. He gives us discernment and revelation. "These things we also speak, not "in words which man's wisdom teaches but which the Holy Spirit teaches, comparing spiritual things with spiritual" (1 Corinthians 2:13). He reveals things to us (2 Peter 1:21). He teaches us all things (John 14:26). We can't navigate our lives without wisdom, discernment, and revelation.

In order to have a successful life, we must be people of the truth. We must have the Spirit of truth in us, teaching us what is true and what is not. We don't want to be people who are "always learning and never able to come to the knowledge of the truth" (2 Timothy 3:7).

We need the Spirit of truth to enable us to discern the truth in all situations (John 14:16-17). Being able to discern the truth from a lie is important in every aspect of our lives. How many people have found themselves in bondage, brokenness, and failure, because they could not discern the truth in every situation?

The Holy Spirit of God is also called the Comforter (John 14:26 KJV), the Spirit of grace (Hebrews 10:29), the Spirit of life (Romans 8:2), the Spirit of adoption (Romans 8:15), and the Spirit of holiness (Romans 1:4). He is eternal (Hebrews 9:14), omnipresent (Psalm 139:7-10), omnipotent (Luke 1:35), and omniscient (1 Corinthians 2:10-11). The Holy Spirit gives you a life of meaning and fulfillment. He builds you up, guides you, makes God's Word alive for you, and by His power enables you to accomplish what you could never do without His help. How could anyone live without Him?

⤳ Prayer Power ⤶

Lord, it is so good to be in Your presence, where everything makes sense. It's wonderful to be home again with You in prayer. When I am with You I feel Your peace, love, and joy rise in me. When I have not spent enough time with You, I greatly miss that priceless sense of the fullness of Your presence.

Lord, I come before You and ask You to fill me afresh with Your Holy Spirit today. Cleanse me with Your living water. Wash away anything in my heart of doubt, fear, or worry. Take away everything in me that is not of You. Enable me to walk in the Spirit and not the flesh, and exhibit the fruit of Your Spirit (Galatians 5:16-17). Do a complete work in me so that I can show Your pure love to others.

Teach me everything I need to know about You. Enable me to exhibit faithfulness, gentleness, and self-control (Galatians 5:22-23). You are the Spirit of wisdom, grace, holiness, and life. You are the Spirit of counsel, might, and knowledge (Isaiah 11:2). Spirit of truth, help me to know the truth in all things.

Thank You for leading and guiding me. Thank You for being my Helper and Comforter. Thank You that Your Spirit within me enables me to walk in Your ways and do Your commands (Ezekiel 36:27). Help me to pray powerfully, and worship You in a way that is pleasing to You. Thank You that You will raise me up to be with You when my life on earth has ended. Until then, lead me ever closer to You.

In Jesus' name I pray.

✣ WORD POWER ✣

I will put My Spirit within you and cause
you to walk in My statutes, and you will
keep My judgments and do them.

EZEKIEL 36:27

When He, the Spirit of truth, has come, He will
guide you into all truth; for He will not speak on
His own authority, but whatever He hears He
will speak; and He will tell you things to come.

JOHN 16:13

I will pray the Father, and He will give you another
Helper, that He may abide with you forever—the Spirit
of truth, whom the world cannot receive, because
it neither sees Him nor knows Him; but you know
Him, for He dwells with you and will be in you.

JOHN 14:16-17

Repent, and let every one of you be baptized in
the name of Jesus Christ for the remission of sins;
and you shall receive the gift of the Holy Spirit.

ACTS 2:38

As many as are led by the Spirit of God, these are
sons of God. For you did not receive the spirit
of bondage again to fear, but you received the
Spirit of adoption by whom we cry out, "Abba,
Father." The Spirit Himself bears witness with
our spirit that we are children of God.

ROMANS 8:14-16

→ 4 ←

Take God at His Word

———◦═◦═◦———

Knowing God doesn't happen without knowing what His Word says about Him. God's Word helps you to understand what works in life and what doesn't. Obedience to God's Word begins by being determined to make no compromise with His ways. It requires a clear understanding that God's rules and laws are for your benefit, and so you do all you can to live by them. When you live this way, every step of obedience you take brings you closer to the freedom, wholeness, and true success God has for you.

My life has never been easy. When you don't have a mother guiding you, and your father is just trying to cope with a mentally ill wife, and you are isolated from other family members who perhaps could have helped but were busy with their own lives and just not around, you grow up having to learn many lessons the hard way. That means making countless wrong choices because you don't know any better, and then paying the consequences.

Learning the hard way how life works has only one advantage I can see. And that is, I learned the lessons well enough to pass them along to others with some credibility. That's because I have been there, lived it, and have the scars to prove it. But I experienced too much needless suffering and pain because I didn't know the right things to do. And I was too naive to see disaster coming. If I had known the Lord at an early age, learned God's ways, and was being led by the Holy Spirit, I would never have done the wild, foolish, and dangerous things I did. I needed an understanding of God's Word long before I had it. I want to tell you what I wish I had known then.

Learn to Take God at His Word

You need to know that you are a slave to whomever you obey. If you obey God's rules, you become a slave of righteousness. If you give yourself over to a life of disobedience to God's ways, you become a slave of sin. "Do you not know that to whom you present yourselves slaves to obey, you are that one's slaves whom you obey, whether of sin leading to death, or of obedience leading to righteousness?" (Romans 6:16).

Some people think they are entirely liberated when they live opposed to God's ways, but the truth is they become a slave to their lifestyle and are not liberated at all. But we *can* be delivered from slavery to sin and become a slave of righteousness where there are countless rewards (Romans 6:17-18).

In order to do that, we need to realize that we cannot obey God's laws on our own. We are too weak. Even when we want to do the right thing, we don't always do it. And often we end up doing the things we don't want to do. The apostle Paul said, "The good that I will to do, I do not do; but the evil I will not to do, that I practice" (Romans 7:19). Even someone as strong in the faith as Paul was—who had seen Jesus, I might add—struggled with this.

After we receive the Lord, we have this inner conflict between our old sinful nature and our new redeemed self. Our flesh wants what it wants, while our mind wants to serve God's laws. Jesus said, "Why do you call Me 'Lord, Lord,' and not do the things which I say?" (Luke 6:46). If we call Jesus "Lord," it is our responsibility to learn right from wrong. And only by reading God's Word can we see what we do wrong. And although we can choose to do what is right, it is the power of the Holy Spirit that enables us to actually do it.

Jesus liberates us from our old self and frees us to dwell in the power of the Holy Spirit. *We* choose to read God's Word and pray that the

Holy Spirit will make it come alive in our heart and enable us to live God's way.

A FEW GOOD REASONS TO
LET GOD'S WORD LIVE IN YOU

To have your prayers heard. "One who turns away his ear from hearing the law, even his prayer is an abomination" (Proverbs 28:9).

To have your prayers answered. "If you abide in Me, and My words abide in you, you will ask what you desire, and it shall be done for you" (John 15:7).

To stay away from trouble. "When the whirlwind passes by, the wicked is no more, but the righteous has an everlasting foundation" (Proverbs 10:25).

To be healed and delivered. "He sent His word and healed them, and delivered them from their destructions" (Psalm 107:20).

To be on a path that leads away from death. "In the way of righteousness is life, and in its pathway there is no death" (Proverbs 12:28).

To receive all God has for you. "For the LORD God is a sun and shield; the LORD will give grace and glory; no good thing will He withhold from those who walk uprightly" (Psalm 84:11).

To have peace. "Great peace have those who love Your law, and nothing causes them to stumble" (Psalm 119:165).

To prosper and be successful. "This Book of the Law shall not depart from your mouth, but you shall meditate in it day and night, that you may observe to do according to all that is written in it. For then you will make your way prosperous, and then you will have good success" (Joshua 1:8).

To have food for your soul. "Man shall not live by bread alone, but by every word that proceeds from the mouth of God" (Matthew 4:4).

To experience God's presence. "LORD, who may abide in Your tabernacle? Who may dwell in Your holy hill? He who walks uprightly, and works righteousness, and speaks the truth in his heart" (Psalm 15:1-2).

It is extremely important to understand that reading God's Word doesn't make us righteous. Our righteousness comes only through faith in Christ (Philippians 3:9). You are considered righteous by God because of what Jesus has done, not by anything you have done. Jesus took on your sin so that you can take on the righteousness of God. "He made Him who knew no sin to be sin for us, that we might become the righteousness of God in Him" (2 Corinthians 5:21).

It is imperative that you *absolutely* know this, because righteousness cannot be obtained by trying to be perfect in carrying out God's laws. We are all doomed for failure if we do that, and eventually people walk away from God because it's miserable to always feel like a failure. You must realize and acknowledge that God sees the righteousness of Jesus in you. But you do have a part in this. He expects you to *want* to live His way from now on. The good news is that the Holy Spirit *in* you carries out the work of living God's way in your life.

Love the Law of the Lord

King David—who was as great a sinner as anyone—said, "I rejoice at Your word as one who finds great treasure. I hate and abhor lying, but I love Your law" (Psalm 119:162-163). "My soul keeps Your testimonies, and I love them exceedingly" (Psalm 119:167). David loved the law of the Lord. He also said,

> The law of the LORD is *perfect*, converting the soul; the testimony of the LORD is *sure*, making wise the simple; the statutes of the LORD are *right*, rejoicing the heart; the

commandment of the LORD is *pure,* enlightening the eyes
(Psalm 19:7-8, emphasis added).

I first fell in love with God's Word shortly after I became a believer.
The Holy Spirit brought it to life in my heart as I read it. Plus, I was
hearing it taught every week by a great Bible teacher. I loved that God's
Word made sense and that my life worked better when I lived by it. I
could feel it changing my heart and mind every time I read it. And I
found that the more I heard it or read it, the more I loved it.

The Bible will do the same for you.

Every time you read God's Word, the Holy Spirit will illuminate it
to your soul, and you will be continuously renewed. It will soften the
places in your heart that have become hard. It will help to transform
you into the person God created you to be. You will become more
and more able to resist the ways of the world that are in opposition to
God's ways.

Every time you read the Bible, your relationship with the Lord will
strengthen and your faith will grow. You will sense the presence of the
Holy Spirit leading you and speaking to your heart as He renews your
mind and reveals truth to you. You will have greater clarity, renewed
hope, and deeper peace. You will become more like Christ. And you
will love God and His Word more.

The Bible is God's ultimate authority on all that has to do with your
life. The specific direction you walk in, the decisions you make, or the
actions you take must all line up with God's Word. Jesus said the truth
will set you free (John 8:32). But not just any truth. You can know
the truth about your finances, your health, your marriage, your relationships, your work situation, the economy, or your government and
never get free. Only the truth of God's Word can make you free.

God's Word is our greatest weapon of spiritual warfare. It is called
"the sword of the Spirit" (Ephesians 6:17). We must read it, speak it,
and believe it in order to stand against enemy attack. Nothing will penetrate our heart and change our lives more profoundly. God's Word
never fails. We must trust it. When we don't have the Word of God

etched in our heart, we run after things that won't fulfill us. We do wrong things that mess up our lives. We live our own way and blame God because our life isn't working. Without God's Word, we end up searching for love and fulfillment in all the wrong places. We end up learning lessons the hard way.

⤳ Prayer Power ⤲

Lord, I am grateful for Your Word. It shows me how to live, and I realize that my life doesn't work if I'm not living Your way. Help me to understand all I read in Your Word. Meet me there in the pages and teach me what I need to know. "Open my eyes, that I may see wondrous things from Your law" (Psalm 119:18). Speak to me and reveal the things I need to know.

Thank You for the comfort, healing, deliverance, and peace Your Word brings me. It is food for my starving soul. Help me to read it every day so that I have a solid understanding of who You are, who You made me to be, and how I am to live. My delight is not in the counsel of the ungodly, but it is in Your law. Help me to mediate on it every day and night so that I can be like a tree planted by a river that brings forth fruit and doesn't wither, so that whatever I do will prosper (Psalm 1:1-3).

Help me to never turn away from Your law. May Your words live in me so that when I pray, I will see answers to my prayers (John 15:7). Enable me to live Your way so that my prayers are always pleasing in Your sight (Proverbs 28:9). Thank You that Your Word reveals what is in my heart. I pray that You will cleanse my heart of all evil and expose anything that is not Your will for my life. Teach me the right way to live so that my life will work the way You intend for it to do.

In Jesus' name I pray.

✦ WORD POWER ✦

The word of God is living and powerful, and
sharper than any two-edged sword, piercing
even to the division of soul and spirit, and
of joints and marrow, and is a discerner of
the thoughts and intents of the heart.

HEBREWS 4:12

The grass withers, the flower fades, but
the word of our God stands forever.

ISAIAH 40:8

Blessed is the man who walks not in the counsel of the
ungodly, nor stands in the path of sinners, nor sits in
the seat of the scornful; but his delight is in the law of
the LORD, and in His law he meditates day and night.
He shall be like a tree planted by the rivers of water,
that brings forth its fruit in its season, whose leaf also
shall not wither; and whatever he does shall prosper.

PSALM 1:1-3

I will worship toward Your holy temple, and praise
Your name, for Your lovingkindness and Your truth; for
You have magnified Your word above all Your name.

PSALM 138:2

Heaven and earth will pass away, but My
words will by no means pass away.

LUKE 21:33

5

MAKE WORSHIP A HABIT

I can't begin to number the times I have gone to church and sung songs of worship and praise along with the other people there, and in the process I felt the hardness of my heart soften, my negative attitude change, and pure joy rise up within me. Actually, I had never known joy until the day I experienced it in worship. I sensed the presence of the Holy Spirit, and I had such a deep awareness of the love of God that it moved me to tears. The joy of the Lord rose in my heart like a sunrise—healing, edifying, engulfing, enlarging, calming, securing, and redeeming.

I knew from that day on my life would never be the same. I was addicted to God's presence. I could not—nor did I want to—live without that joy in my heart. I never wanted to spend a day without His presence manifesting profoundly in my life. The presence of God—and all that He is—overwhelmed me. It didn't matter what I had done or what my circumstances were. It was the only time in my life, until that point, that I had felt unconditional love.

I have experienced that same sense of God's presence many times since then, and each time has been life changing. But I will always cherish the memory of the first time—coming out of the darkness of my past and the negative habits of thought that threatened to derail my life and into the all-encompassing light of the Lord.

You need that same experience too. You must be able to lay down your concerns and troubles and be in the presence of God, letting His love wash over you and fill you with His peace and joy.

The Purest Prayer of All

My definition of prayer is simply communicating with God. It follows, then, that the purest form of prayer is praise and worship. It's pure because the focus is entirely on the Lord and not on us. In worship, we draw close to God—just to be with Him alone—and we communicate our reverence, love, thankfulness, devotion, and praise to Him.

The Bible says that God lives in the praises of His people. "You are holy, enthroned in the praises of Israel" (Psalm 22:3). When we worship Him, His presence comes to dwell with us in a powerful way because praise and worship invite His presence. We are never closer to God than when we worship Him. He is Immanuel, which means "God with us." He *wants* to be with *us*. But *we* must first want to be with *Him*. We show that we want to be with Him every time we worship Him.

The greatest gift we have is the presence of God. It changes everything in our lives. It changes our heart, mind, attitude, and even our circumstances. That's because it is not possible to be in the presence of God and not experience positive change. The reason for that is we become like what we worship (Psalm 115:4-8). The more we worship God, the more we become like Him.

In order to find freedom, wholeness, and true success in life, we must become more like the Lord. And that means spending time in His presence by making praise and worship a way of life.

Most people don't worship God as much as they should because they don't know Him well enough. They don't fully understand all the reasons He is worthy of praise. Nor do they realize the immense impact praise and worship have on their lives. But if you ask God every day to give you a new revelation of who He is, He will do that. And I guarantee that the more you know of Him, the more you will want to praise Him.

Worship and praise are the very means God uses to transform our lives. That's because a gift from God is hidden within our worship of Him. God doesn't need our praise to feel better about Himself or to affirm to Himself that He is God. He already knows He is God, and He doesn't have any doubt about that. The purpose of praise and worship is not to remind God of who He is. It's to remind *us* of who He is. *We* are the ones who need to be reminded.

The precious gift God gives us when we worship Him is more of Himself. When we open up our hearts to Him in praise, He pours Himself into us. He pours His love, peace, power, joy, goodness, wisdom, holiness, wholeness, and freedom into us every time we worship Him.

So, whenever you feel the need for more of the Lord in your life—whenever you need more peace, power, love, joy, or wisdom—worship God.

God created you to worship Him. It is what you were born to do. It's the place you will find your greatest peace and a sense of purpose. It's where you will see who God really is, and in doing so, you will see who *you* really are as well. But worship must become a way of life, a habit, a decision that has already been made, a part of the fabric of your life, a priority, like the air you breathe.

Not only is it necessary to have personal times of worship, it is also very important to worship together with other believers. Powerful things happen in corporate worship. An igniting sense of revival in your soul will melt your heart. Healing happens in His presence, and you will experience greater clarity of mind. You will feel enriched, renewed, and revitalized. Praise and worship are also weapons of warfare because they can reverse what is being set in motion by the enemy.

Ongoing worship in your heart will change everything—especially when it is your *first* reaction to the things that happen, whether good or bad. The more you know who God is, the more you will want to worship Him. The more you know of what God has done, the more you will give Him praise.

When You Want to Be Inspired to Worship

When you want a great incentive to worship, read all of Psalm 103.

Below are just a few verses from that chapter to pique your interest. If you don't find a reason to worship God in any of these verses, then ask God to give you a great awakening.

> Bless the LORD, O my soul; and all that is within me, bless His holy name! (verse 1).

> Bless the LORD, O my soul, and forget not all His benefits (verse 2).

> Who forgives all your iniquities, who heals all your diseases (verse 3).

> Who redeems your life from destruction, who crowns you with lovingkindness and tender mercies (verse 4).

> Who satisfies your mouth with good things, so that your youth is renewed like the eagle's (verse 5).

> The LORD executes righteousness and justice for all who are oppressed (verse 6).

> The LORD is merciful and gracious, slow to anger, and abounding in mercy (verse 8).

> He has not dealt with us according to our sins, nor punished us according to our iniquities (verse 10).

> For as the heavens are high above the earth, so great is His mercy toward those who fear Him (verse 11).

> As far as the east is from the west, so far has He removed our transgressions from us (verse 12).

Finding Transformation in Worship

I love the story in the Old Testament where the people who were carrying the ark of the covenant containing the Ten Commandments stopped every six steps to worship God (2 Samuel 6:13). I am so impressed with that. I believe this is something we must do as well. We should stop often to worship God, whose Holy Spirit of truth we carry inside of us. We should not allow ourselves to go too far without that intimate contact with the Lord.

Whenever you feel overwhelmed by what you are carrying, go before God in praise and worship and He will take your burden away. When you cannot take another step—or feel you cannot do what you need to do—it's probably because you are trying to do it in your own strength. As you worship and praise God, He will strengthen you. And you will have a greater sense of His power and your dependency on Him. God wants you to simply worship Him in the midst of whatever situation you are facing and then trust that He will enable you to do what needs to be done.

The more you know of God, the more you will want to worship Him. In fact, you will not be able to stop yourself.

Praise strengthens and transforms your soul (Psalm 138:1-3). It takes away fear (Psalm 34) and doubt (Psalm 27). It releases the power of God in your life (Psalm 144), and destroys the enemy's plans (Psalm 92). That's because worship and praise put up a protective covering through which the enemy cannot penetrate. This is just the beginning of what God will pour into your life when you worship Him. How can you find true success in life without worshipping the One who makes it all happen?

✦ PRAYER POWER ✦

Lord, I enter Your gates with thanksgiving and Your courts with praise (Psalm 100:4). I worship You as the almighty, all-powerful God of heaven and earth, and the Creator of all things. I praise You as my heavenly Father, who is with me every day to guide and protect me. Thank You for all You have given me and all You will provide for me in the future. "You guard all that is mine. The land You have given me is a pleasant land" (Psalm 16:5-6 NLT).

I praise You for Your love that liberates me and makes me whole. Pour Your love into me so that it overflows to others and glorifies You in the process. Thank You for Your greatest act of love—sending Your Son to die for me. I praise You, Jesus, my Lord and Redeemer, that You have saved me and given me a foundation that is unshakable. "You enlarged my path under me, so my feet did not slip" (2 Samuel 22:37). It is my greatest privilege to exalt You above all and proclaim that You are King of kings and Lord of lords. No one is greater than You.

I praise You for Your Holy Spirit, who leads and comforts me. I praise You for Your wisdom and revelation. I praise You for Your peace and joy. Thank You that You are in charge of my life and nothing is too hard for You. Thank You for enabling me to do what I could never *do* without You. Lord, help me to worship You in ways that are pleasing in Your sight. You are holy and worthy of all praise, and I exalt You above all else.

In Jesus' name I pray.

✤ WORD POWER ✦

The hour is coming, and now is, when the true worshipers will worship the Father in spirit and truth; for the Father is seeking such to worship Him.

JOHN 4:23

Oh, that men would give thanks to the LORD for His goodness, and for His wonderful works to the children of men!

PSALM 107:8

Make a joyful shout to the LORD, all you lands! Serve the LORD with gladness; come before His presence with singing.

PSALM 100:1-2

I will bless the LORD at all times; His praise
shall continually be in my mouth. My
soul shall make its boast in the LORD; the
humble shall hear of it and be glad.

PSALM 34:1-2

You are a chosen generation, a royal priesthood, a
holy nation, His own special people, that you
may proclaim the praises of Him who called you
out of darkness into His marvelous light.

1 PETER 2:9

6

PRAY AS THOUGH YOUR LIFE DEPENDS ON IT

Shortly before Thanksgiving last year, my sister, Suzy, was diagnosed with breast cancer. The news shocked and devastated her husband and children, as well as me and my husband and children. She is such an important part of all our lives that the grief settled on us like a cold lead blanket. We couldn't stop crying, even waking in the middle of the night to cry and pray. We prayed for days and still could not rise above the devastating news.

Five days later my sister, her daughter, Stephanie, our dear friend Roz, my daughter, Amanda, and I all met for prayer. We went into my office on the top floor of our house, where we all meet for prayer every week. We had heavy hearts, and a spirit of grief had settled upon us. Even with all our praying during the previous days, we had not been able to get on top of it at all.

In that prayer meeting, we did as we always do and read the Word first, and then we had a time of worship. After that we prayed for two hours. When the meeting was over, we had a *profound sense* of God's presence, and the spirit of grief was completely gone. Each of us had gained a deep understanding that God had His hand on Suzy and would be with her through this entire process. We all felt there would be victory, not only as the ultimate outcome, but along the way as well. Not one of us could have conjured up those feelings on our own. We knew God had done a work in our hearts in response to worship and prayer.

We walked into that room with grief and sadness, and we walked out with the peace of God. We all had a sense that Suzy would survive and thrive. Even though we didn't know what was ahead, we were certain that God was walking with her through it. We felt a peace that passes all human understanding. We knew God had worked a miracle in our hearts.

Two days before Christmas, Suzy had a double mastectomy. The doctor told her that the cancer had not spread and she would not have to have any further treatment. This was fantastic news for all of us and the greatest gift we could have been given. It was the best of all possible outcomes, but even if the news had not been so positive, we knew that God would have seen her through each step of treatment too. We would have continued to pray for healing and still maintained the peace God gave us that day.

James, one of Jesus' brothers, said, "Is anyone among you suffering? Let him pray" (James 5:13). He also said, "You do not have because you do not ask" (James 4:2). It can't get any clearer than that. We have to pray.

Talking about prayer again, James said, "You ask and do not receive, because you ask amiss, that you may spend it on your pleasures" (James 4:3). Prayer has to be more than just asking for things we want. It is, first of all, the means by which we get close to God and spend time with Him and talk to Him and listen to Him. It's how we get to know Him better and show our love to Him. It's waiting at His feet so we can find freedom and healing in His presence. Prayer is the means by which we acknowledge our dependence upon Him and our gratefulness for His power in our life.

I have personally seen countless answers to prayer for my marriage, children, health, emotions, mind, work, and much more. I have seen answers to prayer that at the time I didn't know were even possible. I am certain that God answers prayer, and I want you to know that too. It is absolutely crucial for every aspect of your life.

Resisting the Temptation to Not Pray

If all these things James said about prayer are true—which I believe they are, because the Bible was divinely inspired by God—then what is our problem? What make us hesitate to pray? Why don't we pray enough, even when we know we should and really do want to? Here are some possible reasons why we don't pray as much or as fervently as we should:

- We don't fully believe what God's Word says about prayer.

- We suspect the Bible was written for everyone else but us.

- We think we're too busy.

- We don't believe God will hear our prayers and answer them.

- We don't feel we're good enough to deserve an answer to prayer.

- We want God to do what we want without any effort on our part.

- We've seen instances where God did not answer a prayer, and therefore we concluded that God doesn't answer *any* prayer.

- We think we can make life work on our own.

- We imagine God surely has far better things to do than answer our prayers.

- We believe Jesus was talking about prayer only to His disciples and no one else on the planet.

- We don't have enough faith to believe that prayer works.

- We think we don't know how to pray.

- We believe we can't face God after we have failed again to live His way.

- We forget that we have the Holy Spirit in us as a direct line to God, helping us to pray.

- We're intimidated by all the great prayers we've heard others pray, and we fear we won't sound eloquent enough.
- We don't look at prayer as a dialogue with God, so we see our prayers as never rising above the ceiling, let alone to God's ears.

If you relate to any of these reasons for not praying enough, you are not alone. There are many people who feel that way. In fact, I believe this feeling is epidemic. But the good news is you can *pray* about *praying,* and God will enable you to pray more and better.

Not knowing how to pray is a nonissue if your definition of prayer is simply communicating with God. When you pray, you are sharing your heart with Him. That means there is no wrong or bad prayer, only honest prayer. If you're thinking, *My concerns are not important enough for God to waste His time answering,* let me assure you that God has plenty of time. Actually, He has all the time in the world. And everything that is important to you is important to Him. Just as a good father or mother will listen to their son or daughter talk about something that is important to their child, God listens to you.

If you think, *I can't come crying back to God after I've failed again,* please know that we all have times of failure. Even after we receive Jesus, and He has forgiven us of all our past sins, we can still sin again. God knows that about us, and it's why He gave us confession and repentance as a way to clear the slate. Remember that the enemy wants you to feel condemnation because he knows that will keep you from going before God. Don't give him the satisfaction.

If you are thinking, *I don't feel as though I am good enough for God to even listen to my prayers, let alone answer them,* then welcome to the family. Most of us feel that way. But that's not a bad thing. Let me explain this receiving Jesus process again.

When you receive Jesus, from then on God sees the righteousness of Jesus in you. He sends the Holy Spirit to live in you, and now you can be close to God. You can speak to Him and hear Him speak to your heart. The Holy Spirit helps you to pray, and God hears and answers, not because of what you deserve, but because of what *Jesus* did.

It's called grace.

None of us are good enough to deserve all that God has for us. It's Jesus *in* us that makes us good enough. You have to understand this, or the enemy will come in with his lies to convince you otherwise, and this may keep you from praying.

What Jesus Said About Prayer

———

Ask, and it will be given to you; seek, and you will find; knock, and it will be opened to you. For everyone who asks receives, and he who seeks finds, and to him who knocks it will be opened (Luke 11:9-10).

When you pray, go into your room, and when you have shut your door, pray to your Father who is in the secret place; and your Father who sees in secret will reward you openly (Matthew 6:6).

Whatever things you ask in prayer, believing, you will receive (Matthew 21:22).

Whatever you ask in My name, that I will do, that the Father may be glorified in the Son. If you ask anything in My name, I will do it (John 14:13-14).

Pray for Your Needs and the Needs of Others

The way you learn to pray is by praying. Jesus taught us to pray for our needs in the Lord's Prayer. He never said *don't* pray for your needs. He said God knows what you need, so don't worry about it—pray instead. Not worrying about something doesn't mean you don't pray about it. It means you pray about it and trust God to answer in His way and His time. Start with the most pressing needs on your heart. Then pray for the needs of everyone around you in your life and in your world. Ask God to show you what the true needs are.

The other day my daughter shared with me how she prayed with a friend who had come to her specifically for prayer. This friend shared something very serious and tragic that had happened, and how in a terribly damaging way it had affected his life since then. Amanda had to pray powerful prayers for deliverance far beyond her comfort zone and experience—and her friend was set free from the stronghold of sadness that had invaded and gripped his life for so long. She would have probably hesitated to do that if she'd not been in a prayer group for years. She was glad she'd had the experience of praying in front of others and was able to meet this crucial challenge. She learned that the more you pray, the more effective your prayers are.

Don't pass up any opportunity to pray for others. Everyone needs prayer, and they won't care how eloquent you sound.

When God Has Not Answered Your Prayer

If you have prayed about something and you haven't seen an answer yet, remember that prayer is not telling God what to do. Prayer is telling God what you *want* Him to do and then putting it in His hands and waiting on Him to do what *He* wants.

King David, a man after God's own heart, struggled with his own unanswered prayers. He wondered how long he would be sorrowful because God seemed to not hear him. In the end he decided to trust God's mercy and praise Him for all the good things He had done for him (Psalm 13). We, too, need to trust in God's mercy and praise Him for all the good things He has done in our lives.

Being mad at God for not answering your prayer is not a good way to live. It's like boarding up the door on a grocery store in the midst of a famine. It's like biting the hand that feeds you. It's like turning your back on the only possibility you have of experiencing a miracle. It would be better to go before the Lord, praising Him as the almighty, all-powerful, all-knowing God of the universe who supplies your every need.

As you worship God, you grow in faith that He is greater than anything you are praying about. This helps you trust that He knows what you need and will answer your prayers in *His way* and *His time*. Trusting Him opens your eyes to see that even when the things you are praying about seem hopeless and dire, God has the power to change everything. You will have strength to keep praying and not stop too soon.

Praying is sharing your heart with God and telling Him everything. It's not that He doesn't already know these things. He does. It's that He wants to hear about them from *you*. That's because He wants you to depend on Him. He has sovereignly set it up that *you* pray and then *He* moves in response to your prayers. God wants you to have a life of freedom, wholeness, and true success, but none of that can happen if you are not praying.

✦ Prayer Power ✦

Dear Lord, teach me to pray. Help me to pray about not just *my* needs but also the needs of others. Show me how to pray about everything.

I cry out to You and declare my trouble before You (Psalm 142:1-2). Enable me to "pray without ceasing" (1 Thessalonians 5:17). Help me to leave the things I pray about at Your feet and in Your hands. Teach me to trust You so much that I don't have preconceived ideas about the way my prayers must be answered. I know it is my job to pray and Your job to answer. Help me to do my job and let You do Yours.

Help me to trust that You will answer in Your way and in Your time. I confess any time that I have made demands, expecting You to answer my prayers the way I wanted You to. I know that Your will and Your judgments are perfect, and so I will praise You above all things—even my own desires and expectations. You are my Resting Place and the Solid Rock on which I stand. Nothing will shake me, not even seemingly unanswered prayers. When I can't see the answers to my prayers, open my eyes to see things from Your perspective. "I will lift up my eyes to the hills—from whence comes my help? My help comes from the LORD, who made heaven and earth" (Psalm 121:1-2).

Lord, I am grateful that You, who are the all-powerful, all-knowing God of the universe, are also my heavenly Father, who loves me unconditionally and will never forsake me. Thank You for hearing and answering my prayers.

In Jesus' name I pray.

⇢ WORD POWER ⇠

For the eyes of the LORD are on the righteous,
and His ears are open to their prayers; but the
face of the LORD is against those who do evil.

1 PETER 3:12

I cry out to the LORD with my voice; with my
voice to the LORD I make my supplication.
I pour out my complaint before Him; I
declare before Him my trouble.

PSALM 142:1-2

If you have faith and do not doubt...if you
say to this mountain, "Be removed and
cast into the sea," it will be done.

MATTHEW 21:21

Continue earnestly in prayer, being
vigilant in it with thanksgiving.

COLOSSIANS 4:2

They cried out to the LORD in their trouble,
and He saved them out of their distresses.

PSALM 107:19

7

LIVE IN THE FREEDOM GOD HAS FOR YOU

Finding the freedom God has for you means separating yourself from anything that separates you from God. It means getting free of whatever holds you back from becoming all He made you to be. It also means being liberated from anything that keeps you from moving into all God has planned for your life.

Living in freedom involves receiving deliverance from such things as anxiety, fear, addictions, depression, obsessive behavior, bad attitudes, and the traps and consequences of sin. We are all walking on a narrow path, longside which are dangerous traps we can fall into. We can be deceived and get off the path by buying into lies the enemy throws our way, and end up living with things from which God wants us to be free. Sometimes we have lived so long with certain habits, thoughts, and feelings that we accept those things as *us*. We think, *This is just the way I am* or *This is how life is*. We don't realize that those are things from which we can be liberated.

God wants to transform us all from the inside out. That's why Jesus came as the Deliverer. He didn't come as the *precursor* to FedEx. He came as the *curser* of evil, from which He wants to deliver anyone who receives Him as Savior.

What Is Deliverance?

Deliverance is the cutting loose from anything that controls you other than God. If anything in your life has control over you—such as an eating disorder, addictions of any kind, compulsive behavior, fear, or gripping negative emotions—you need to be free of that because it is hindering all God wants to do in you. (More about that in chapter 19, "Refuse Negative Emotions.")

Deliverance releases you to become who you really are—it doesn't change you into something else. When you receive deliverance from the Lord, you won't say, "I don't know who I am anymore." You'll say, "Now I know who I really am." You will not lose yourself; you will *find* yourself. And you will like what you see. What God made you to be is good, because He desires that you become more like Him and *He* is good.

Deliverance sets us free from anything negative in our past that still has influence into our lives. If you have any memories from the past that have a negative effect on your life now, you need to be delivered from them. Even a cruel or insensitive word spoken to you yesterday that makes you feel bad today means you need to be set free from it. God wants you to be liberated from anything that keeps you from moving into all He has for you.

Deliverance was a regular part of Jesus' ministry. When Jesus said, "All things are possible to Him who believes," He was specifically talking about being delivered from evil spirits (Mark 9:23). But deliverance is not limited to that. We often need to be set free from our own bad habits of thought and action. If there wasn't a need for deliverance, why would Jesus have come as the Deliverer? And why did He set so many people free and tell others that they would be able to do the same or even greater things?

Deliverance happens in many ways. You can find deliverance and freedom in prayer. You can also find it in the presence of God when you are in worship. Deliverance can happen as you are reading the Word of God and He opens your eyes to see His truth about your situation. It can occur when someone prays for you. It can also manifest during or after a time of fasting and prayer.

I found freedom from depression and anxiety after fasting for three days and being prayed for by others. I have found freedom from fear after reading God's Word every time I felt afraid. I have found freedom from obsessive thought patterns, negative emotions, and a bad attitude while I was in a time of worship and praise. I have been set free from bad eating habits involving a preoccupation with specific foods—such as sugar, which is like a poison for me—as I fasted and prayed. I have been set free from temptation, which I knew was a trap of the enemy to destroy me, by going into my prayer closet and laying prostrate on the floor before the Lord and praying that He would break that assignment from hell.

I have been set free from unforgiveness so many times over the years I can't begin to count them. God always wants us free from that debilitating thought process. Unless we live as a recluse and have no interaction with anyone else, there will periodically be someone we need to forgive for something. The moment you detect unforgiveness in your heart, know that God is waiting to set you free from it.

How Do We Find Freedom?

It is important to remember that even though we are not specifically choosing the enemy's path, we can still end up on that path if we are not intentionally and deliberately choosing the will of God.

For that reason, in order to find freedom you must choose to confess each sin, to pray about and reject each temptation, to bring concerns to God *before* they get out of control, and to ask God to deliver you from any stronghold the enemy is trying to erect in your life. Ask God to wash you clean with the flow of His Spirit, so that there is nothing in your mind and soul that is polluting. Ask Him to help you stay in His perfect will in all you do.

Far too often we are living with things we shouldn't. When you have anger that is hard to control or bad habits you cannot break, or you can't stop from thinking about something negative that has happened or something you fear *might* happen, you must go to the Lord and ask Him to set you free. If you are unable to forgive someone, or you feel distant from God, can't make decisions, or find it too hard to do constructive things, then you need deliverance. Don't live with these conditions, because Jesus paid the price for you to be free of them. Choose to do whatever is necessary in order to be liberated.

Choose to Obey God's Laws

You can become burdened by bondage if you continually allow yourself to disobey God. Choosing to live God's way can set you free.

Choose to Have a Clean Heart

During times of great disappointment, tragedy, or trauma, when negative emotions such as anger, fear, hatred, or unforgiveness go unconfessed, your heart can be gripped by emotions that are not God's will for your life. Bring all that to God and ask Him to set you free from it.

Choose to Cry Out to the Lord for Freedom

God is always waiting for us to come to Him, so we can be set free from anything that keeps us from becoming more like Him. To the children of Israel in bondage in Egypt, God said He saw their oppression, heard their cry, and knew their sorrows, so He came to deliver them (Exodus 3:7-8). He will do the same for you.

Choose to Praise God for Who He Is and What He Has Done

One of the ways we can find freedom and deliverance is to praise God in the midst of our imprisonment. When the apostle Paul was imprisoned, he didn't grumble and complain. Instead, he prayed and lifted up praise to God. "At midnight Paul and Silas were praying and singing hymns to God, and the prisoners were listening to them. Suddenly there was a great earthquake, so that the foundations of the prison were shaken; and immediately all the doors were opened and everyone's chains were loosed" (Acts 16:25-26). Praise opened the prison doors and broke the chains that bound the prisoners. Praise will do that for you today. Praise invites God's presence, and in His presence you will always find liberty.

Choose to Have Faith That Brings Down Strongholds

Having faith in God and His Word is powerful enough to bring down strongholds in your life. "They cried to You, and were delivered; they trusted in You, and were not ashamed" (Psalm 22:5). You can be set free simply by standing on faith in God's Word.

If you have something in your life from which you would like to be free, remember that the power of God—the power of the Holy Spirit in you—is greater than anything you are facing. "He who is in you is greater than he who is in the world" (1 John 4:4). The power of God is far greater than the power of the enemy. Speak to whatever you are struggling with and say, "I will not be controlled by this because God is in control of my life and I submit and surrender to Him."

Don't become discouraged if you feel that you are never going to get completely free of something. Freedom is often a process. There may be many layers to get through. Whether it is a new level of freedom you need, or freedom from the same old thing coming up again, the Bible says that God will continue to deliver you as long as your heart is open to Him working in your life (2 Corinthians 1:10).

If He is not giving up on you, then you shouldn't either.

✦ PRAYER POWER ✦

Lord, I thank You that You are "my fortress, my high tower and my deliverer, my shield and the One in whom I take refuge" (Psalm 144:2). Thank You that "You have delivered my soul from death," and have "kept my feet from falling," so that I may walk before You (Psalm 56:13).

Lord, show me anything from which I need to be set free. Reveal whatever I am not seeing. I don't want to be living with something from which You already paid the price for me to be liberated. I pray that You "will deliver me from every evil work and preserve me" for Your kingdom (2 Timothy 4:18). Bring me "out of the house of bondage" (Exodus 20:2). "O God, do not be far from me; O my God, make haste to help me!" (Psalm 71:12). "You *are* my help and my deliverer; do not delay, O my God" (Psalm 40:17, emphasis added).

I see that the forces rising up against Your believers are powerful, but I know You are far more powerful than they are. I cry out to You to liberate us from the enemy who tries to put us into bondage. I thank You that You will answer by setting us free (Psalm 118:5). Thank You that You will never give up on us but will continue to deliver us (2 Corinthians 1:9-10).

Thank You, Lord, that You will deliver me from all evil and be with me in trouble. To You be glory forever and ever.

In Jesus' name I pray.

✢ Word Power ✦

You are my hiding place; You shall preserve
me from trouble; You shall surround
me with songs of deliverance.

Psalm 32:7

Stand fast therefore in the liberty by which
Christ has made us free, and do not be
entangled again with a yoke of bondage.

Galatians 5:1

The righteous cry out, and the Lord hears, and
delivers them out of all their troubles.

Psalm 34:17

Yes, we had the sentence of death in ourselves, that we
should not trust in ourselves but in God who raises the
dead, who delivered us from so great a death, and does
deliver us; in whom we trust that He will still deliver us.

2 Corinthians 1:9-10

He shall call upon Me, and I will answer him;
I will be with him in trouble; I will deliver
him and honor him. With long life I will
satisfy him, and show him My salvation.

PSALM 91:15-16

8

SEEK GOD'S KINGDOM AND HIS GIFTS

———◦•✦•◦———

A kingdom is a place where a king rules. The kingdom of God is wherever King Jesus rules.

The kingdom of God is where life rules over death, where the kingdom of light rules over the kingdom of darkness, where satanic powers of disease and destruction are overthrown by the rule of God.

When Jesus was crucified and resurrected, He broke all the power of hell and brought the rule of God on earth. And now we not only have life with Him for eternity, but also more life in *this* life. Wherever the kingdom of God is established, the enemy cannot hold us hostage.

When John the Baptist said, "Repent, for the kingdom of heaven is at hand!" he was referring to Jesus, the King of all, who had come to earth to overthrow the forces of hell and defeat the power of evil (Matthew 3:2). Jesus was the long-awaited Messiah—the Deliverer and Savior—who came to bring hope, power, and eternal life to anyone who would receive Him. The kingdom of heaven was near because the King was there.

Jesus said, "The kingdom of God is within you" (Luke 17:21). It is a spiritual kingdom. Jesus said that His kingdom was not of this world (John 18:36). It comes from God, who is in heaven. He also said, "It is easier for a camel to go through the eye of a needle than for a rich man to enter the kingdom of God" (Matthew 19:24). That means it's not possible to trust in the material wealth of this world over God and still expect to enter God's kingdom. Jesus is the King of the kingdom of God. The enemy rules in the material kingdom of money and materialism.

In teaching His disciples the Lord's Prayer, one of the things Jesus said to pray is, *"Your kingdom come.* Your will be done on earth as it is in heaven" (Matthew 6:10, emphasis added). When praying "Your kingdom come," we are asking God to establish His rule within us so that we are entirely submitted to Him. We are also asking Him to establish His kingdom wherever we are. What follows, then, is that God's will is done on earth in the same way it is done without question in heaven.

The kingdom of God rules wherever we, who believe in Jesus, declare His rule. Jesus said that the greatest person in the kingdom of heaven is someone who is humble (Matthew 18:1-4). (Kingdom of God and kingdom of heaven can be used interchangeably.) That means we must be expectant, teachable, free of all arrogance, and submitted to the Lord's will. Jesus said, "I tell you the truth, anyone who will not receive the kingdom of God like a little child will never enter it" (Mark 10:15 NIV).

To seek God's kingdom means we must come humbly before God, knowing that we cannot live without Him and declaring that we depend on Him for everything. The Bible says that God "gives grace to the humble" (James 4:6). Jesus said, "Blessed are the poor in spirit, for theirs is the kingdom of heaven" (Matthew 5:3). Isaiah said, "He gives power to the weak" (Isaiah 40:29). The requirement of humble dependence on God shows up again and again.

Pride is the worst sin because it leads to rebellion against God. Pride caused Satan to rise up and rebel against God, which led to his downfall. Anyone who becomes prideful believes they can handle their life better without God. Those who are humble, on the other hand, recognize that everything they need in life comes from the Lord. Only those who *know* they need the Lord will experience the kingdom of God.

Jesus said that to be great in God's kingdom you must serve others (Luke 22:26). That also takes humility.

The Kingdom of God Is Where God's Gifts Are Found

In God's kingdom are many gifts. The Bible says that every good gift comes from our heavenly Father (James 1:17). In order to receive these gifts, we must first seek God and His kingdom. We need to understand what God's gifts are and open ourselves up to receive them. God wants us to value His gifts enough to seek Him for them. Jesus said, "If you then, being evil, know how to give good gifts to your children, how much more will your Father who is in heaven give good things to those who ask Him!" (Matthew 7:11).

God has many gifts, such as the gifts of salvation, the Holy Spirit, His power, peace, and a sound mind, which are all covered in other chapters. Two of the most important gifts we most often forget are God's *love* and His *grace*. These are gifts we especially need to remember to receive every day. Without them, life does not work.

The Gift of God's Love

One of God's greatest gifts is His love. We cannot survive successfully without it.

What drew me to the Lord in the beginning was the love of God that I sensed in the Christians I knew. When I learned that God loved us before we even knew Him, my heart was smitten. When I realized that He accepts us the way we are, but He loves us too much to leave us that way, I was sold. The Bible says, "Many are the woes of the wicked, but the LORD's unfailing love surrounds the man who trusts in Him" (Psalm 32:10 NIV).

The love of God is not just a feeling or an emotion. It is the Spirit of God in us. When we receive Jesus, we receive the love of God and nothing can change that. The Bible says there isn't anything that will "be able to separate us from the love of God which is in Christ Jesus our Lord" (Romans 8:39). The more you invite God to pour His love into your heart, the more His love will flow through you in greater dimensions and overflow to others.

The Gift of God's Grace

We cannot receive the Lord without the gift of God's grace being extended to us (Ephesians 2:8). Grace is when God doesn't give us the punishment we deserve but instead gives us the good things we *don't* deserve. When we know we don't have something and can't get it on our own, and God gives it to us, that is His grace.

God "gives grace to the humble" (Proverbs 3:34). That means the good things that happen to us don't depend on our efforts, but on our humbly receiving God's mercy and grace (Romans 9:16). Grace is when God takes our weakness and manifests His strength in us (2 Corinthians 12:9). That's how His grace is sufficient for us. He does it and we don't.

Jesus said not to worry about anything because God knows what we need. But He didn't say, "Don't pray about it." He said to *seek God's kingdom first*—which is God's rule in your life—and *seek His righteousness* as well. "Do not worry, saying, 'What shall we eat?' or 'What shall we drink?' or 'What shall we wear?' For after all these things the Gentiles seek. For your heavenly Father knows that you need all these things. But seek first the kingdom of God and His righteousness, and all these things shall be added to you. Therefore do not worry about tomorrow, for tomorrow will worry about its own things. Sufficient for the day is its own trouble" (Matthew 6:31-34).

If we want to live in freedom, wholeness, and true success—which means having everything we need—we must seek God's kingdom rule in our lives above all else.

✢ Prayer Power ✦

Lord, I come humbly before You and seek Your kingdom and Your dominion in my heart and life above all else. May Your kingdom be established wherever I go and in whatever I do. Make me a pure vessel for Your power to go forth and proclaim the rule of King Jesus where You have given me influence to do so.

Thank You, Lord, for Your many gifts to me. Thank You for Your gifts of salvation, justification, righteousness, eternal life, and grace. Thank You for Your gifts of love, peace, and joy. Thank You that these will never fail in my life because You are my everlasting Father and *You* will never fail. Your unfailing love is a great comfort to me (Psalm 119:76 NIV). Thank You that nothing can ever separate me from Your love (Romans 8:35-39).

Thank You for Your grace that gives me far better than I deserve. Thank You, Jesus, for taking the consequences of my sin. Thank You for giving me the mind of Christ and Your wisdom and knowledge of the truth. I pray You will teach me all the "mysteries of the kingdom of heaven" (Matthew 13:11).

Help me to seek Your kingdom every day and live in the gifts You have given me. "For Yours is the kingdom and the power and the glory forever" (Matthew 6:13).

In Jesus' name I pray.

✢ Word Power ✦

Jesus answered and said to him, "Most assuredly, I say to you, unless one is born again, he cannot see the kingdom of God."

John 3:3

Do not fear, little flock, for it is your Father's
good pleasure to give you the kingdom.

LUKE 12:32

To each one of us grace was given according
to the measure of Christ's gift.

EPHESIANS 4:7

Now we have received, not the spirit of the world,
but the Spirit who is from God, that we might know
the things that have been freely given to us by God.

1 CORINTHIANS 2:12

The works of the flesh are evident, which are:
adultery, fornication, uncleanness, lewdness, idolatry,
sorcery, hatred, contentions, jealousies, outbursts
of wrath, selfish ambitions, dissensions, heresies,
envy, murders, drunkenness, revelries, and the
like; of which I tell you beforehand, just as I also
told you in time past, that those who practice such
things will not inherit the kingdom of God.

GALATIANS 5:21

9

MAINTAIN A
RIGHT HEART

We all have a propensity for heart problems. I'm talking about our spiritual heart here, but I imagine our physical heart is affected by our spiritual heart more than we know. We all can look back to times when the condition of our heart—whether good or bad—affected the way we felt in our body. How many of us have become physically ill because we have been heartsick? How many of us have a body that broke down at one time or another because our heart was broken in some way?

Our heart is broken when someone disappoints us, is mean to us, says things that hurt us, or leaves us—whether by death or by their own decision to depart. Our heart can be filled with destructive things, such as anger, hatred, unforgiveness, bitterness, selfishness, or resentment. Our heart can be polluted by the things we see, read, or watch. Our heart is affected negatively when we compromise the ways of God in our lifestyle choices.

Our mind can be tainted by just living in this world and letting it rub off on us. How many times are we shocked to hear profanity on a television program or in a film that is supposed to be "family oriented"?

I recently saw the previews to a film for children that used the Lord's name in vain many times. And for what reason? To make more money, I'm sure. But such a thing pollutes little minds and paves the way for young hearts to be hardened to the things of God.

I will not subject myself to that because I don't want my heart hardened, my mind polluted, and the Holy Spirit within me grieved. Yes, I am an adult and can discern between good and bad. And that's exactly why I make an adult decision to separate myself from all that doesn't glorify the Lord. There is a price to be paid when we *don't* do that, and it's not worth it.

We cannot expect God to make our life work when we're doing things that hinder His work in our lives.

Life works best when the ongoing cry of our heart is like King David's, who said, "Search me, O God, and know my heart; try me, and know my anxieties; and see if there is any wicked way in me, and lead me in the way everlasting" (Psalm 139:23-24). He wanted God to uncover anything in his heart and mind that was ungodly. He desired to live God's way and knew that having a right heart was the key to that.

David also prayed, "Create in me a clean heart, O God, and renew a steadfast spirit within me" (Psalm 51:10). David's main fear—which is my concern as well—is found in the next verse. "Do not cast me away from your presence, and do not take Your Holy Spirit from me" (Psalm 51:11). David wanted a cleansing and renewing of his heart because he did not want to experience the departure of the Holy Spirit from him. He had seen that happen to King Saul—who was king just before David—because of the sinful things Saul had done. David had done some terrible things as well, and his life fell apart. But unlike Saul, David repented of everything and sought to get his heart right with God again.

Because Jesus has come and given the Holy Spirit to those who receive Him, the Holy Spirit doesn't leave us unless we deliberately reject Him. However, we can lose some of the fullness of the Holy Spirit's presence in our lives if we harbor uncleanness in our heart. I know that the Holy Spirit won't leave me, because I am never leaving Him, but I don't want to do anything that will keep the presence of the Holy Spirit from manifesting fully in my life.

God wants your heart to be soft and not hard. He wants you to have a heart that is humble and not full of pride (Proverbs 21:2). He desires that you have a pure heart so you can see Him and His goodness in your life (Psalm 73:1). God gave you a new heart and put a new spirit within you when you received Jesus (Ezekiel 36:26). Now He wants to establish your heart "blameless in holiness" before Him (1 Thessalonians 3:13).

What Can I Do to Maintain a Right Heart?

First of all, you must realize that you cannot hide even a thought from God. "'Can anyone hide himself in secret places, so I shall not see him?' says the LORD; 'Do I not fill heaven and earth?' says the LORD" (Jeremiah 23:24). God sees and knows everything.

Second, you must know that you cannot make your heart as pure and clean as God wants it to be. "Who can say, 'I have made my heart clean, I am pure from my sin'?" (Proverbs 20:9). You must ask God to give you a clean heart and show you what steps to take. The Bible says that "the preparations of the heart belong to man" (Proverbs 16:1). But how do you prepare your heart? Below are some practical suggestions that will help you do that.

Ask God to Reveal the Condition of Your Heart

God knows—and is eager to reveal to you—what is truly going on in your heart. When you ask Him to do that, He will (1 Corinthians 4:5). Ask the Lord to reveal any pride you may have. You don't want to experience the trouble that comes along with it (Proverbs 13:10). That is where so many of our serious problems begin.

Stay in God's Word

The Word of God is referred to as "living," "powerful," "sharper than any two-edged sword," and "a discerner of the thoughts and intents of the heart" (Hebrews 4:12). That means as you read the Bible, what's in your heart will be revealed. God wants "a broken and a contrite heart" (Psalm 51:17). He doesn't want us to harden our hearts against Him in any way.

We harden our heart when we refuse to listen to what He is speaking to us in our times alone with Him in prayer and in His Word. "Today, if you will hear His voice, do not harden your hearts" (Hebrews 4:7). We harden our heart when we see clearly in His Word what we should do and then don't do it. "He who is often rebuked, and hardens his neck, will suddenly be destroyed, and that without remedy" (Proverbs 29:1).

Our heart is hard when we resist God's Word in any way. Jesus had just done a miracle in front of His disciples by taking five loaves of bread and two fish in order to feed 5000 people. Yet the disciples still could not comprehend His power toward them for their own needs. It says of them that "they had not understood about the loaves, because their heart was hardened" (Mark 6:52).

If the disciples, who were *with* Jesus every day and witnessed His many miracles, had hearts that were hardened, how much more so might *we* have a heart that is hardened too? Ask God to soften your heart every time you read His Word.

Get Rid of All Sin in Your Life

Sin is deceiving. Sin tells you it's okay to do what you're doing. Sin tells you, "It's not that bad, and, besides, everybody else is doing it." Sin tells you, "It's *your* life and you can do what you want." Sin in your life reveals where your loyalties are. God looks for the faithful people "to show Himself strong on behalf of those whose heart is loyal to Him" (2 Chronicles 16:9).

Don't allow yourself to become "hardened through the deceitfulness of sin" (Hebrews 3:13). If you allow any sin to reside in your heart, God will not listen to your prayers (Psalm 66:18). Sin will take away your joy (Psalm 51). It will become like a cancer that grows silently, until one day it is discovered and the damage is done.

Keep Your Heart with All Diligence

Your heart cannot be trusted. That's why you must keep a close watch over it (Proverbs 4:23). You cannot assume that nothing bad will ever find a place to reside there. Make a special effort to fill your heart with good treasure. "A good man out of the good treasure of his heart brings forth good things" (Matthew 12:35).

Aside from filling your heart with the Word of God, as I mentioned earlier, fill your heart also with worship and praise, and you will find good treasure there. David said, "To You, O LORD, I will sing praises. I will behave wisely in a perfect way…I will walk within my house with a perfect heart" (Psalm 101:1-2).

He goes on to say something else that is key to maintaining a right heart. "I will set nothing wicked before my eyes; I hate the work of those who fall away; it shall not cling to me. A perverse heart shall depart from me; I will not know wickedness" (Psalm 101:3-4). In other words, David would not allow his eyes to look at evil, he would not tolerate violations of God's laws, he would not allow anything perverse to reside in his heart, and he would refuse all wickedness.

This is a lesson for all of us who want to maintain a right heart before God.

✦ PRAYER POWER ✦

Lord, create in me a clean heart. Set me free from anything that is not of You. Cleanse my heart of all sin and direct it to Your ways (Psalm 119:36). Help me to hide Your Word in my heart so that I will not sin against You (Psalm 119:11).

Keep me always awed by Your Word (Psalm 119:161). I don't want any sin in my heart to hinder my prayers to You (Psalm 66:18). Keep me undeceived (Deuteronomy 11:16). Help me not to foolishly trust my own heart, but instead to trust You to reveal the truth I need to see (Proverbs 28:26). Give me a wise heart so that I can receive all Your commands (Proverbs 10:8).

Holy Spirit, align my heart with Yours. Flush out of my heart all that is dark and wrong and replace it with more of You. Search my heart and make changes wherever they are needed. Soften my heart where it has become hard. Purify my heart where it has become polluted. Help me to set nothing wicked before my eyes.

Lord, I pray You would take away anything in my heart that keeps me from being a full partaker of Your holiness (Hebrews 12:10). Help me to praise You with my whole heart, so that I withhold nothing from You (Psalm 9:1). Teach me to always maintain a right heart before You.

In Jesus' name I pray.

✦ WORD POWER ✦

Blessed are the pure in heart, for they shall see God.
MATTHEW 5:8

If I regard iniquity in my heart, the Lord will not hear.
PSALM 66:18

Take heed to yourselves, lest your heart be
deceived, and you turn aside and serve
other gods and worship them.
DEUTERONOMY 11:16

He who trusts in his own heart is a fool, but
whoever walks wisely will be delivered.
PROVERBS 28:26

Keep your heart with all diligence, for
out of it spring the issues of life.
PROVERBS 4:23

10

Move in Forgiveness— God's and Yours

———————

I n order to enjoy the freedom, wholeness, and true success God has
for you, forgiveness has to flow like liquid in your heart. If you harbor unforgiveness, it stops up the flow of the Spirit in you. It can even
keep your prayers from being answered (Psalm 66:18).

We are supposed to turn our unforgiveness into forgiveness *before*
we even pray. Jesus said, "Whenever you stand praying, if you have
anything against anyone, forgive him, that your Father in heaven may
also forgive you your trespasses" (Mark 11:25). God will withhold His
forgiveness from us as long as we withhold our forgiveness from anyone else.

This is serious business.

If we do not forgive, not only will we have unforgiveness in us
eating away at our mind and body, but we will not enjoy complete
forgiveness from God, which in itself will be a major strain on our conscience. We will lose all peace. It is not worth it just to hang on to a few
moments of inner revenge.

If we don't forgive, the only one being hurt is us. I've said this before,
but it is worth repeating here: *Forgiveness doesn't make the other person*

right, it makes you free. And in order to have wholeness and true success, we have to be free. Forgiveness enables us to move on with our life.

Receive God's Forgiveness

One of the best ways to become a forgiving person is for you to understand and receive God's forgiveness. Forgiveness is what God has chosen to give to you, and He wants you to choose to give it to others. Jesus said, "Forgive, and you will be forgiven" (Luke 6:37). It can't get any clearer than that.

Don't become confused about God's forgiveness. When you receive Jesus, you are completely forgiven of all past sins. The slate is clean. The reason I had to go back and confess certain sins of the past in Mary Anne's office after I had become a believer was because those sins still had a tormenting hold on me. I still had unforgiveness toward my mother. And while I had stopped all my occult practices, I still had many books on the occult sitting in my house. Also, I had not specifically confessed the two abortions I'd had before I became a believer, and even though God had forgiven me of all that when I received Jesus, I still couldn't forgive myself. Confessing those sins helped me receive the forgiveness God had already extended to me, and it also broke the consequences of sin I had allowed to pervade my life.

Remember, God has given you a way to receive His full forgiveness, and that is to confess the sin and repent of it. You say, "I did this, Lord, and I ask You to forgive me. I hate what I have done and am so deeply sorry about it that I intend to never do it again." However, if we want God to forgive *us* of everything, *we* also have to forgive.

The only way to receive God's forgiveness for our unforgiveness is to forgive others completely.

Refuse to Get Stuck in Unforgiveness

Not forgiving others is one of those self-torturing sins. It may feel good for a moment, but soon it will begin to destroy you. Don't allow yourself to do it. Instead, obey God by letting people off the hook. Give them a chance to change and be different than what they were. That doesn't mean you have to set yourself up to be hurt again. It means you release them into God's hands and you get on with your life.

Whenever you forgive someone, you gain greater freedom, wholeness, and true success. That's because when you forgive, you are stepping into the river of life, where you are refreshed and cleansed. When you forgive, you become more like the Lord. When you don't forgive, unforgiveness takes over your life. While unforgiveness doesn't take away your salvation, it does limit what God can do in you and through you. It keeps you from becoming all you can be.

Ask God to show you anyone you need to forgive. Believe me, when you pray this way, God will bring that person quickly to mind. It may be from your distant past or as recently as yesterday. It may be someone you didn't realize you needed to forgive, but when that person comes to your mind, you will know why. Whoever or whatever it is that needs your forgiveness, confess it before God and ask Him to help you forgive completely. Refuse to hold anyone to yourself by not forgiving him (her). Release that person to God and ask Him to work complete forgiveness in your heart. I have found that turning people over to God in prayer and asking Him to work in their lives to bring them into right alignment with Him is better than revenge. God will answer that prayer and you will be released in the process.

Forgiveness doesn't always happen overnight. Often it's a process—especially for deep and damaging hurts. If you have forgiven someone and the next day you feel the same unforgiveness, hurt, anger, and bitterness against him (her), don't be discouraged or think nothing has changed. Sometimes it takes layers of forgiveness to strip away the layers of unforgiveness that have accumulated over time. Continue to pray and ask God to help you forgive completely.

Be especially diligent to forgive both your parents and your spouse. Carrying unforgiveness toward any one of them will bring misery and grief into your life. Ask God to show you if you have any resentment in that area. Even with the best of people in the best of circumstances, there can still come times when we need to forgive.

I have found that if you pray often for the person you need to forgive, it softens your heart toward him (her). The truth is that you always grow to love the person you pray for. And that's because you develop God's heart of love for him or her in the process.

If you need to ask for forgiveness *from* someone, ask God for guidance about how to approach him or her and the timing of it. Cover it in prayer first. Then proceed as you feel led by the Holy Spirit. Whether or not that person will forgive you is something you cannot control. Just know that you have done the right thing and can now move on.

The willingness to forgive is something we must keep ready in our hearts every day. That doesn't mean we allow people to be hurtful or destructive toward us. Enabling them to do evil is not right either. It means that we have decided we are not going to harbor unforgiveness and allow it to turn into bitterness. We have the power to make a decision to not live with unforgiveness in our heart.

When we confess our unforgiveness, that clears the air between us and God. The Bible says, "If our heart does not condemn us, we have confidence toward God. And whatever we ask we receive from Him, because we keep His commandments and do those things that are pleasing in His sight" (1 John 3:21-22). That is more than enough promise for me. Having a clear conscience and a confident mind allows us to stand before God, knowing we are obeying Him and are pleasing in His sight. And then we know He will hear our prayers and answer them. That is incentive enough to keep my heart and mind fully forgiving all the time. What about you?

Step out of the pit of unforgiveness and step into the cleansing stream of forgiveness—God's and yours.

⤖ Prayer Power ⬾

Lord, I thank You for forgiving me and not even remembering my sins anymore (Hebrews 8:12). Show me anything I need to confess to You today so that I can bring it before You and be set free. Convict my heart any time I stray from Your laws and commandments.

I especially ask that You would reveal any place in my heart where I have not forgiven someone. I don't want to harbor anything within me that will keep my prayers from being heard. I don't want to live in unforgiveness anymore, for any reason. Help me to be a forgiving person in the same way You are forgiving toward me. Help me to always forgive quickly and not wait for the other person to say or do what I think they should.

Show me any way I need to ask someone to forgive me so that we both can be healed and set free. If I have hurt someone without realizing it and there is unforgiveness in his (her) heart, reveal that to me so I can make amends. If I have been selfish with anyone, and that has diminished the way that person feels about himself (herself), enable me to clear the air between us.

Lord, take away anything of anger, bitterness, or resentment in my heart. Pour out Your Spirit upon me and cleanse me of all that is not of You. Enable me to be a person who lives in the forgiveness You have given me so I can extend forgiveness freely toward others (Ephesians 4:32).

In Jesus' name I pray.

✢ WORD POWER ✦

Judge not, and you shall not be judged.
Condemn not, and you shall not be condemned.
Forgive, and you will be forgiven.

LUKE 6:37

He who loves his brother abides in the light, and
there is no cause for stumbling in him. But he
who hates his brother is in darkness and walks in

darkness, and does not know where he is going,
because the darkness has blinded his eyes.

1 John 2:10-11

Be kind to one another, tenderhearted, forgiving
one another, even as God in Christ forgave you.

Ephesians 4:32

If you bring your gift to the altar, and there
remember that your brother has something
against you, leave your gift there before the
altar, and go your way. First be reconciled to your
brother, and then come and offer your gift.

Matthew 5:23-24

If you forgive men their trespasses, your
heavenly Father will also forgive you. But if you
do not forgive men their trespasses, neither
will your Father forgive your trespasses.

Matthew 6:14-15

⇥ 11 ⇤

FEAR GOD, BUT
DON'T LIVE IN FEAR

———◆◗◉◗◆———

You don't have to live in fear. Even though there is much to be afraid of in this world, you don't have to spend your life fearing what could happen.

When we see frightening events occurring around us, plus the many corrupt and dangerous things we observe some people engaged in, those things cause us to think to ourselves, *Are these people crazy? Don't they see what they are doing and what the consequences will be?*

The answers to these questions are *yes,* people act crazy when they have no godly wisdom; and *no,* the godless are unable to weigh the consequences of what they are doing. They do foolish things because they have no sense of what is right. The description of a fool is a person who cannot see the consequences of his behavior. Fools do not have the fear of God, and therefore they have no restraints. Wisdom and understanding of the consequences of our actions come from having a fear of God.

Having the fear of God means you have such a love and reverence for God that you are afraid of what life would be like without Him.

Some people believe there is no God. Others think there might be a God, but they refuse to acknowledge Him in their lives because they certainly don't want Him telling them how to live. They want to do what they want to do. This is what the Bible says about such people, "There is none who seeks after God. They have all turned aside; they have together become unprofitable; there is none who does good, no, not one...Destruction and misery are in their ways; and the way of peace they have not known. There is no fear of God before their eyes" (Romans 3:11-12,16-18).

In contrast to that, having the fear of the Lord causes a person to do the opposite. It causes them to seek God and His truth, to do what's right, to promote life, to build up and not tear down, to bring peace, and to run from evil.

We live in a culture that can be poisonous. God's ways are mocked and sin is glorified. All we have to do in order to slide backward is do nothing. We don't have to seek out evil; it seeks *us* out. Evil presents itself, and we have to choose to turn away from it. We have to control our thoughts and what we view and listen to. We have to turn away from ungodliness and turn toward God. We must ask the Lord to put godly fear in our hearts to keep us on the right path. "I will make an everlasting covenant with them, that I will not turn away from doing them good; but I will put My fear in their hearts so that they will not depart from Me" (Jeremiah 32:40).

We have to say, "Lord, put Your fear in my heart so that I will not depart from You in any way."

What Happens When You Have the Fear of God?

God provides a place of refuge that takes away your human fear. "In the fear of the LORD there is strong confidence, and His children will have a place of refuge" (Proverbs 14:26).

God gives you the desires of your heart. "He will fulfill the desire of those who fear Him; He also will hear their cry and save them" (Psalm 145:19).

God blesses you and your children in every way. "Blessed is the man who fears the LORD, who delights greatly in His commandments. His descendants will be mighty on earth; the generation of the upright will be blessed. Wealth and riches will be in his house, and his righteousness endures forever" (Psalm 112:1-3).

God gives you a life of fulfillment and peace. "The fear of the LORD leads to life, and he who has it will abide in satisfaction; he will not be visited with evil" (Proverbs 19:23).

God helps you live His way. "Blessed is every one who fears the LORD, who walks in His ways" (Psalm 128:1).

God delivers you from your enemies. "But the LORD your God you shall fear; and He will deliver you from the hand of all your enemies" (2 Kings 17:39).

God watches over you. "Behold, the eye of the LORD is on those who fear Him, on those who hope in His mercy" (Psalm 33:18).

God helps you walk away from evil. "In mercy and truth atonement is provided for iniquity; and by the fear of the LORD one departs from evil" (Proverbs 16:6).

God reveals all you need to know. "The secret of the LORD is with those who fear Him, and He will show them His covenant" (Psalm 25:14).

God gives you everything you need. "Oh, fear the LORD, you His saints! There is no want to those who fear Him. The young lions lack and suffer hunger; but those who seek the LORD shall not lack any good thing" (Psalm 34:9-10).

God keeps your life from being shortened. "The fear of the LORD prolongs days, but the years of the wicked will be shortened" (Proverbs 10:27).

God sends His angel to free you from harm. "The angel of the LORD encamps all around those who fear Him, and delivers them" (Psalm 34:7).

Having the fear of God doesn't mean you will be shaking under your bed because you're afraid God is going to strike you with lightning. Godly fear comes from a deep reverence and love for Him. It's something *He* puts in your heart when you turn to Him, and it will bless and protect you. The fear of God is something we all must desire.

What the Bible Says About Fear That Is Not from God

There is a type of fear we do *not* want. And God doesn't want it for us, either. Being afraid is draining and exhausting, and it takes away peace, joy, energy, concentration, and productivity from our lives.

The truth is, however, that when you have the fear of God, you don't have to live in fear of anything else. When you make the Lord your refuge—the source of your life—He protects you. In fact, God says that we are to immerse ourselves in His love, which dissolves all fear, trusting that He will keep us safe. When we are afraid, we can go to God and He will take away all fear. "Because you have made the LORD, who is my refuge, even the Most High, your dwelling place, *no evil shall befall you,* nor shall any plague come near your dwelling" (Psalm 91:9-10, emphasis added).

God says that fear does not come from Him. "God has not given us a spirit of fear, but of power and of love and of a sound mind" (2 Timothy 1:7). Paul even refers to fear as "the spirit of bondage again to fear" (Romans 8:15). He said we didn't receive that kind of fear either, but what we *did* receive is "the Spirit of adoption." We have been adopted by our heavenly Father and we have nothing to fear. The spirit of fear comes from the enemy and is something from which we can be set free.

I am not talking about when you have brief moments of fear and then you are over it. When a spirit of fear grips you, you can feel it engulfing you like a cold sheet around your back. It's always there, lurking in your mind. The only way I know to break the hold of it is to stand on God's Word and proclaim the truth—that God did not give you a spirit of fear; He gave you His love and His power. He also gave you a sound mind so that you can *choose* to live in His love and power. You can reject a spirit of fear.

I used to be gripped and nearly paralyzed by fear.

When I was 14, I was babysitting for a family with six children. They lived three houses down and across the street from our house. It was on a corner lot, so the back of their house faced toward my house. The children were very well behaved, or I would never have been able to handle six at once. One night after the parents had left and the four younger children were in bed, I was sitting at the dining table talking to the two older children—a boy about eight and a girl about ten—when we heard what sounded like someone rattling the door handle in the kitchen. The three of us looked at one another in alarmed silence and listened for a moment. Then suddenly we heard the lock in the door-knob unmistakably click open.

The three of us ran with lightning speed to the parents' bedroom, and I grabbed the phone and dialed my mother. While I told her what had just happened, the young boy peeked out the bedroom door into the living room and saw a man coming toward us. He came clear into the hall while I was still on the phone, and I believe when he heard me hysterically telling my mother to come quickly, he turned and ran out of the house.

While I dialed the police, my mother walked down the sidewalk toward the house where we were, but still on the opposite side of the street. Suddenly she saw a man come running out the backyard gate. She stopped and stood very still in the shade of a large tree so that the streetlights would not reveal she was there. She saw that this man was wearing only a shirt that hung down about halfway to his knees and no pants. She watched him go a few feet into the alleyway, in back of the house where I was with the children, where he stopped and put on the pants he must have stashed there. Then he took off running down the alley. My mother came into the house through the open kitchen door and back to where we were still hiding in the bedroom. I had never been so grateful to see her.

Two days later, a man matching the same description as the one who broke into that house where we were also broke into a home one street over from ours and killed a little boy. That man had escaped from a nearby mental hospital just a short time before he broke into the place where I was babysitting. I cried and cried. It still makes me cry to think about it today. I cry for how close we came to disaster. And I cry for that little boy and his parents.

From that time on, I greatly feared being alone. I had a tormenting fear of someone breaking into my home. It wasn't until I came to know Jesus, and had the perfect love of God healing me, that the fear disappeared. It's not there anymore. I think about the possibilities for dangerous situations, but they no longer grip my life. I take precautions and don't do anything stupid to invite trouble, but my reverence for God has made me confident that He is with me to protect me. I think He was with me back then. Even though I didn't know Him, I did have a praying grandmother.

THREE THINGS TO REMEMBER
ABOUT UNGODLY FEAR

1. *The presence of God will be with you to keep you from fear.* "Yea, though I walk through the valley of the shadow of death, I will fear no evil; for You are with me; Your rod and Your staff, they comfort me" (Psalm 23:4).

2. *The promises of God will empower you to reject fear.* "Fear not, for I am with you; be not dismayed, for I am your God. I will strengthen you, yes, I will help you, I will uphold you with My righteous right hand" (Isaiah 41:10).

3. *The love of God will take fear away.* "There is no fear in love; but perfect love casts out fear, because fear involves torment. But he who fears has not been made perfect in love" (1 John 4:18).

The fear of God in your heart will keep you from entertaining destructive behavior. It will prevent you from disobeying God's laws—

and the government's too. It will cause you to turn away from anything offensive that grieves the Holy Spirit in you. The fear of God will steer you away from any foolish thoughts, actions, or words. It will stop you from planning to do anything opposed to God's ways. The fear of God will cause your life to work the way it is supposed to.

Who doesn't need that?

⇁ PRAYER POWER ⇽

Lord, I revere You in every way. Enable me to show my love and adoration for all that You are. "Teach me Your way, O LORD; I will walk in Your truth; unite my heart to fear Your name. I will praise You, O Lord my God, with all my heart, and I will glorify Your name forevermore" (Psalm 86:11-12). Help me to give the glory due You at all times, for I worship and praise You above all else.

I bring all my fears to You and ask You to take them from me so that I no longer live in fear of anything. You are "my light and my salvation" and "the strength of my life. Of whom shall I be afraid?" (Psalm 27:1). I know You have not given me a spirit of fear; You have given me love, power, and a sound mind. In Your presence all my fear is gone, for Your love takes it away.

Help me to make praise my first reaction to fear whenever it comes upon me. I don't want to deny Your presence by giving place to fear in times of weakness. Enlarge my faith to extinguish all fear so that I can trust in Your Word and Your power to protect me. Your Word that says "though an army may encamp against me, my heart shall not fear" (Psalm 27:3). How grateful I am that when I cry out to You, You hear me and deliver me from all my fears (Psalm 34:4).

I know that reverence of You brings life and keeps me away from the pitfalls that lead to death (Proverbs 14:27). Enable me to have that godly fear in my heart always. I don't want to sacrifice any of the blessings, protection, wisdom, fulfillment, peace, and long life that You have for those who fear You.

In Jesus' name I pray.

✦ WORD POWER ✦

The fear of the LORD is a fountain of life, to
turn one away from the snares of death.

PROVERBS 14:27

Though an army may encamp against me, my
heart shall not fear; though war may rise
against me, in this I will be confident.

PSALM 27:3

By humility and the fear of the LORD
are riches and honor and life.

PROVERBS 22:4

As a father has compassion on his children, so the
LORD has compassion on those who fear him.

PSALM 103:13 NIV

The mercy of the LORD is from everlasting
to everlasting on those who fear Him, and
His righteousness to children's children.

PSALM 103:17

→ 12 ←

REPLACE DOUBT WITH UNWAVERING FAITH

———⋅◦✶◦⋅———

We all have faith in something. If we didn't have faith in anything, we wouldn't even get out of bed in the morning. We have faith that we can make it to the kitchen without the roof falling in on us. We have faith that we can get to the store without being killed. We have faith that the doctor is not going to prescribe something that will destroy our body. We have faith that when we go to work we are actually going to get paid. We have faith that when we go to a restaurant we are not going to be poisoned. (And I have said many times that some restaurants require more faith than others.) Our lives would be miserable if we had no faith in anything.

Faith is a choice.

Faith in God is a choice too. We choose to believe God exists and that His Word is true. That means we choose to believe *His good news* in the face of any bad news in our life. We choose to believe that God can do what He promises and refuse to doubt that, no matter what our circumstances are telling us. We choose to believe that the power of God is greater than anything we face. Those are choices we need to make every day.

What we must *not* do is put faith in our faith. Our faith doesn't accomplish anything by itself; *God* accomplishes everything. You have faith in God when you pray, and *He* responds to your prayer. Your faith doesn't *make* God respond to your prayers; your faith *invites* God to work powerfully in your life.

Understanding this is extremely important because we can't get where we need to go in life without faith in God. Faith in His power enables us to go beyond anything we could do on our own. And it keeps us from trying to do everything by our own efforts. We make a decision whether to trust only in ourselves or in our all-powerful God.

Even having faith comes as a gift from God. "God has dealt to each one a measure of faith" (Romans 12:3). But we have to grow it. And that happens every time we read, speak, or hear His Word. Your faith increases according to how much you read the Bible. "Faith comes by hearing, and hearing by the word of God" (Romans 10:17).

The Enemy of Faith

The enemy of faith is doubt, of course, but doubt is also something we have control over. We can choose to reject our own doubt. And that's what we must do if we want to make our life work.

This is something we too often forget.

When doubt comes upon us, we can act as though we have no choice but to entertain it. But we *do* have a choice. We can refuse it. No matter how faith filled we are, doubt can creep up on us in weak moments, such as when we are afraid, overtired, or experiencing strife, or when bad things happen through no fault of our own. Doubt can also begin to overtake us when we spend too much time around faith-less people who have no absolutes and who question the things of God—not for the purpose of finding answers, but rather to under-mine the faith of other people. This can open the way for doubt to creep into our mind.

But you have a choice. Whenever you have doubt about God's ability to protect and provide, you can deliberately say, "I refuse to allow doubt to set up camp in my soul." Then name the things you have doubt about. Read the Word of God until you have evidence in the Scriptures that refutes those doubts and establishes your faith again. I am telling you that this is a big issue in finding true success for your life. And it's not living in denial. Actually, *not* having faith is living in denial—it's denying the truth and power of God and His Word.

Below is a short list of what I am talking about. Remember that the Scriptures are not just words—they have *life.* The Holy Spirit in you breathes life into the Holy Spirit-inspired words of the Bible so that as you read them they come alive in your heart. Here are just a few examples of how to reject doubt and put faith in God.

My Reason to Have Doubt:	**God's Reason to Have Faith:**
"I feel weak and doubt I can handle what I am facing."	"I can do all things through Christ who strengthens me" (Philippians 4:13).
"What just happened to me is a disaster, and I don't see how I recover from it."	"All things work together for good to those who love God, to those who are the called according to His purpose" (Romans 8:28).
"I am afraid of what could happen."	"Perfect love casts out fear" (1 John 4:18).
"I don't know if God will answer my prayers."	"If you ask anything in My name, I will do it" (John 14:14).

The Choice Is Yours

Faith is a spiritual choice. Doubt is a choice of the flesh.

The carnal side of you is not subject to God. It wars against God until you make a decision to bring your flesh under control. But we don't always see doubt as a choice. While it's true that there are times we all doubt, we don't have to live with it. We can choose to have faith in God and His Word.

Simon Peter was one of the trusted disciples who had been with

Jesus all along and saw Him do miracles. Jesus told Peter that Satan wanted to test him, but that He had prayed Simon Peter's faith would not fail (Luke 22:31-32). How much more should we pray that same way for ourselves?

Whenever you have doubt, confess it to God as sin. "Whatever is not from faith is sin" (Romans 14:23). Read in the Word about the men and women of faith. Their stories will inspire you. Abraham waited years for God to fulfill His promise to him about having a son. In the time of waiting, his faith grew stronger and not weaker. It says of Abraham that "he did not waver at the promise of God through unbelief, but was strengthened in faith, giving glory to God" (Romans 4:20). Pray that you can have faith that doesn't falter but only grows stronger as you wait on God to answer your prayers.

Feeling weak, or being aware of your inabilities or limitations, does not indicate a lack of faith. Feeling that God is weak toward you, or that He has limitations, is a lack of faith.

Ask God to help you be so strong in your faith that you will strengthen the faith of others around you who might themselves be struggling. Ask Him to give you faith strong enough to take you where you need to go. The Israelites couldn't enter the Promised Land because of their lack of faith (Hebrews 3:19). Let's learn from them and not allow doubt to keep us from all God has for us.

Life doesn't work if you put your faith in the wrong things. You can never experience all the freedom, wholeness, and true success God has for you without faith in Him and His Word.

⇥ PRAYER POWER ⇤

Jesus, You are "the author and finisher" of my faith (Hebrews 12:2). Thank You for the gift of faith You have given me. Increase my faith every day as I read Your Word. Give me strong faith to believe for the answers to my prayers. I know that it is not about me trying to establish great faith on my own, but that faith comes from Your Spirit and Your Word.

Help me to trust You with all my heart and not rely on my own understanding. I acknowledge You in all my ways and depend on You to direct my path (Proverbs 3:5-6). Help me to trust You in all things every day. Keep me from doubting You and Your Word. I know that "whatever is not from faith is sin," so I confess all doubt within me (Romans 14:23). Your Word says that anyone who doubts is unstable and double-minded and cannot please You (James 1:6-8). I pray You would make me to be strong in faith that pleases You.

Lord, You are everything to me. I know that because of You I am never without love, joy, hope, power, protection, and provision. Because of You I can rise above my limitations and live in peace, knowing You will work things out for my good as I live Your way. Help me to read Your Word every day. Open my eyes more and more to Your truth. Enable me to recognize and understand Your promises to me so that I can daily choose to reject all doubt in my life.

In Jesus' name I pray.

✦ WORD POWER ✦

Without faith it is impossible to please Him, for he who comes to God must believe that He is, and that He is a rewarder of those who diligently seek Him.

HEBREWS 11:6

Let him ask in faith, with no doubting, for he who doubts is like a wave of the sea driven and tossed by the wind. For let not that man suppose that he will receive anything from the Lord; he is a double-minded man, unstable in all his ways.

JAMES 1:6-8

Having been justified by faith, we have peace
with God through our Lord Jesus Christ.

ROMANS 5:1

For a little while, if need be, you have been grieved
by various trials, that the genuineness of your
faith, being much more precious than gold that
perishes, though it is tested by fire, may be found
to praise, honor, and glory at the revelation of Jesus
Christ, whom having not seen you love. Though
now you do not see Him, yet believing, you rejoice
with joy inexpressible and full of glory, receiving
the end of your faith—the salvation of your souls.

1 PETER 1:6-9

I have been crucified with Christ; it is no longer I
who live, but Christ lives in me; and the life I live
which I now live in the flesh I live by faith in the Son
of God, who loved me and gave Himself for me.

GALATIANS 2:20

13

Welcome God's Will and Do It

There are two good ways to understand the will of God for your life: One is to read God's Word, and the other is to pray.

Reading God's Word every day will help you understand what is *always* God's will for your life. And then by *doing* those things you know are *always* God's will, a foundation is laid that enables you to discover what the specifics of God's will are for your own personal life. For example, it is always God's will for you to praise Him. The more you worship and praise God, the more you will gain an understanding about the details of His will for you personally.

Things That Are Always the Will of God for Your Life

It is always God's will for you to acknowledge Him in every way. "In all your ways acknowledge Him, and He shall direct your paths" (Proverbs 3:6).

It is always God's will for you to live by faith. "Now the just shall live by faith; but if anyone draws back, My soul has no pleasure in him" (Hebrews 10:38).

It is always God's will for you to worship Him. "You shall worship the Lord your God, and Him only you shall serve" (Matthew 4:10).

In addition to finding God's will in His Word, you must also pray to receive the knowledge, wisdom, and insight you need personally in order to walk in the right direction.

Seventeen years ago my husband and I sought to know God's will about whether we should move from Los Angeles, California, to Nashville, Tennessee. We found pros and cons in both directions. Many people said the decision was obvious, but half of them thought we should stay in L.A., and the other half thought it was obvious we should move to Nashville.

My husband was drawn to Nashville and I wanted to stay in L.A. What convinced me that a move to Nashville was the wrong step was the way my husband reacted to me when I had hesitation about it. I thought if he were being led by the Holy Spirit regarding this move, he wouldn't be angry and demanding. I knew we needed to surrender our dreams to God and pray for clear knowledge of His will.

Michael prayed that if we were supposed to move, God would speak to *my* heart about it too. I had to fast and pray many times about this, fully wanting to do God's will, but always hoping I wouldn't have to move and leave my family, close friends, and church home that I loved. It took months, but then one day God suddenly dropped revelation into my heart, and I knew it was the will of God that we make the move.

It was important for us both to have certainty that this was God's will because there was nothing easy about the move or the adjustment that followed. In fact, relocating across the country was extremely difficult. Being in God's will doesn't mean things will be easy. Just ask Jesus. He was in God's will when He went to the cross.

Michael and I knew we had done the right thing when, just months after we moved to Tennessee, our California house was destroyed in the Northridge earthquake. We had not sold it yet, but we knew we were supposed to move when we did. And it was a good thing that we followed the Lord's leading, because it would have been an even worse disaster had we been there at the time. The earthquake insurance we had only covered half of what we paid for the house, so we lost a great deal financially. But we would have lost so much more—possibly even our lives—had we ignored the will of God and stayed there.

We all need to know the will of God concerning specific details of our lives. "Should I go there or stay here?" "Should I take this job or that one?" "Can I trust this person or not?" The good news is that we can start immediately toward that end by doing what we *know is definitely* the will of God. For example, while it is not God's will for everyone to move to Nashville, it *is* God's will for us to pray that He will lead us where He wants us to be.

WHY YOU MUST DESIRE
THE WILL OF GOD

To enter the kingdom of God. "Not everyone who says to Me, 'Lord, Lord,' shall enter the kingdom of heaven, but he who does the will of My Father in heaven" (Matthew 7:21).

To live with God forever. "The world is passing away, and the lust of it; but he who does the will of God abides forever" (1 John 2:17).

To avoid living in the lust of the flesh. "He who has suffered in the flesh has ceased from sin, that he no longer should live the rest of his time in the flesh for the lusts of men, but for the will of God" (1 Peter 4:1-2).

To receive the promise of God. "You have need of endurance, so that after you have done the will of God, you may receive the promise" (Hebrews 10:36).

To avoid unnecessary suffering. "It is better, if it is the will of God, to suffer for doing good than for doing evil" (1 Peter 3:17).

HOW TO FIND
THE WILL OF GOD

Tell God you live to do His will. "Bondservants, be obedient...not with eyeservice, as men-pleasers, but as bondservants of Christ, doing the will of God from the heart" (Ephesians 6:5-6).

Ask God for wisdom to help you understand what His will is. "Do not be unwise, but understand what the will of the Lord is" (Ephesians 5:17).

Ask God to enable you to do His will. "May the God of peace... make you complete in every good work to do His will, working in you what is well pleasing in His sight, through Jesus Christ, to whom be glory forever and ever" (Hebrews 13:20-21).

Listen for God's voice speaking to your heart. "Your ears shall hear a word behind you, saying, 'This is the way, walk in it,' whenever you turn to the right hand or whenever you turn to the left" (Isaiah 30:21).

Praise God and give thanks to Him for everything. "In everything give thanks; for this is the will of God in Christ Jesus for you" (1 Thessalonians 5:18).

Ask God to work His will in your life for His glory. "Looking unto Jesus, the author and finisher of our faith, who for the joy that was set before Him endured the cross, despising the shame, and has sat down at the right hand of the throne of God" (Hebrews 12:2).

Once You Know What to Do, Do It

Once you know what the will of God is, it's very important that you do what He is telling you to do.

Jeremiah was angry with the people of Israel because they asked him to pray that they would know God's will about whether to stay where they were or go to Egypt. He did pray and received the answer, but the people didn't do what God instructed them to do.

Jeremiah said to them, "You were hypocrites in your hearts when you sent me to the LORD your God, saying, 'Pray for us to the LORD our God, and according to all that the LORD your God says, so declare to us and we will do it.' And I have this day declared it to you, but you have not obeyed the voice of the LORD your God, or anything which He has sent you by me. Now therefore, know certainly that you shall die by the sword, by famine, and by pestilence in the place where you desire to go to dwell" (Jeremiah 42:20-22).

Praying to know God's will and then not doing it has very serious consequences—in this case, horrible suffering and death. Not living in the will of God after He reveals it to you opens a pathway for much suffering to come into your life as well. Choosing to live in the will of God can help you dwell away from unnecessary trouble and premature death.

I am not saying that anyone in the will of God will never experience suffering and death. Jesus will tell you that is not true. He was in the will of God when He went to the cross, but there was great purpose in His suffering and sacrifice. And that will be true for you also. If you are in the will of God and something bad happens, you can trust that God has a plan to bring good out of what is occurring.

After Jeremiah prayed that prayer, the answer didn't come for ten days. Even though Jeremiah had a direct line to God and God's favor, he still had to wait for the answer. You, too, have a direct line to God— His name is Jesus—and you have favor with God because of Him. So if you are praying about which way to go, or what decision to make, don't grow impatient while waiting on the Lord for the answer. Remember that you are on *God's* timetable; He is not on yours.

The problem with the Israelites was that they had already made up their minds as to what they were going to do, even before they asked God. So it didn't matter that God told them to stay where they were and not go to Egypt; they were determined to go anyway. As a result, they were destroyed, all because they wouldn't listen to God and obey His will for their lives.

When we ask God for direction, we have to be willing to obey it once we know what it is. The consequences for not doing so are serious.

Jonah is another great example of the consequences of not doing God's will once you know what it is. God told Jonah to go to a certain place, and he not only refused to do it, he ran from the presence of the Lord. He boarded a ship headed to a place where he must have mistakenly believed he could escape from God. Then came a terrible storm and Jonah was tossed overboard into the sea, where he was swallowed by a great fish. He stayed in the belly of that fish for three days and nights, which gave him a lot of time to think. From this hopeless place Jonah prayed and worshipped God. He was then restored to dry land. When God again told Jonah where He wanted him to go and what to do, he did it.

There is much more to this great story that is well worth reading again and again, but for the purpose of this chapter, suffice it to say that it is better to do God's will than it is to be swallowed up by the consequences of *not* being in His will. "'When I called, they did not listen; so when they called, I would not listen,' says the LORD Almighty" (Zechariah 7:13 NIV).

Jesus, by great contrast, said, "I do not seek My own will but the will of the Father who sent Me" (John 5:30). When He was facing the cross, He fell on His face before God and prayed, "O My Father, if it is possible, let this cup pass from Me; nevertheless, not as I will, but as You will" (Matthew 26:39). Jesus wanted God's will more than His own life.

When Jesus taught His disciples how to pray, He instructed them to say, "Your will be done on earth as it is in heaven" (Luke 11:2). That is how we must pray as well. No matter what *we* want, we must want what *God* wants more.

✧ Prayer Power ✧

Lord, I pray You would teach me to do Your will (Psalm 143:10). Work the desire for Your will into my heart (Philippians 2:13). Help me to "stand perfect and complete" in Your will and stay in the center of it at all times (Colossian 4:12).

I am grateful to You that Your will can be known. I seek to know Your will for my life today. Guide my every step so that I don't make a wrong decision or take a wrong path. "I delight to do Your will, O my God" (Psalm 40:8). Fill me with the knowledge of Your will in all wisdom and spiritual understanding (Colossians 1:9).

Line the desires of my heart up with the desires of Your heart. I want what You want for my life. Help me to refuse to hold on to things that are not of You. Help me to cling to You instead of my own dreams. I only want to do Your will from my whole heart (Ephesians 6:6). When I experience difficult times, help me to know if it is because I have done something wrong, or if it is that I have done something right and this is happening according to Your will (1 Peter 4:19).

Lord, only You know what is right for me. Help me to hear Your voice leading me. Transform me to do Your will (Romans 12:2). Help me to have endurance so that I can do Your perfect will and receive the promises of all You have for me.

In Jesus' name I pray.

✧ Word Power ✧

For this reason we also, since the day we heard it, do
not cease to pray for you, and to ask that you may be
filled with the knowledge of His will in all wisdom and
spiritual understanding; that you may walk worthy of

the Lord, fully pleasing Him, being fruitful in every
good work and increasing in the knowledge of God.

COLOSSIANS 1:9-10

This is the confidence that we have in Him, that if
we ask anything according to His will, He hears us.

1 JOHN 5:14

Whoever does the will of My Father in heaven
is My brother and sister and mother.

MATTHEW 12:50

Let those who suffer according to the will
of God commit their souls to Him in
doing good, as to a faithful Creator.

1 PETER 4:19

This is the will of God, that by doing good you
may put to silence the ignorance of foolish men.

1 PETER 2:15

14

Recognize Your Purpose and Work to Fulfill It

Not having a sense of purpose in life is a dangerous thing. We can end up making wrong choices, doing stupid things, becoming frustrated or unfulfilled, and falling into traps of the enemy. Granted, we can still experience any of these same things even when we *do* have a sense of purpose, but at least it's not a chronic situation. It's a temporary deviation from a general path—where we stumble briefly on the road of our life—but then, because we *do* have a sense of purpose, we quickly straighten up and head in the right direction again.

Having a sense of purpose doesn't mean you know every detail of your future. You may actually know very few details about it. In fact, you may not know at all where the road that God has you on will take you. But you *do* know where it will *not* take you. For example, you may sense that you are called to use your gifts to help people, but you know you are not called to leave your spouse and children to do that. This knowledge alone will help you make certain right decisions.

Having a calling or a sense of purpose will stop you from crumbling when you face fear or failure. It will keep you moving on when you become discouraged. It will prevent you from wasting valuable time doing something that you know is not right for you. People who throw away their life with drugs, alcohol, gambling, or viewing pornography have no idea of God's purpose for them. If they did, I believe their God-given sense of purpose would quickly override their desire for all that. Their calling would call them away from it—or could have prevented it from happening in the first place. Even when a person is a victim of something horrendous, he or she needs to understand that the high purpose of God has not been lost; it is still there. I believe not having that sense of purpose is an underlying factor in the serious problems many people face.

I am convinced that all the trouble and heartbreak I experienced in the years before I became a believer were because I didn't have Jesus or the Holy Spirit in me or a sense of God's purpose for my life. The only sense I had about anything was that life is fragile, it could all be over in an instant, that every day is a struggle to survive, that I am powerless to change myself or anything about my life, and that the people who are supposed to love you don't, unless you can be and do what they want you to be and do.

But after I became a believer, I finally had a sense of hope and purpose. The most valuable thing in my life was the loving, accepting, rejuvenating, strengthening, freeing, healing, restoring presence of God. It was like nothing I had ever experienced. It was unmistakable. Every time I walked into church I sensed that strong presence, and it would bring me to tears. Not tears of bitterness, sadness, frustration, or self-pity as before, but tears that washed away a lifetime of all that. They were tears that healed, cleansed, restored, repaired, and softened my heart where it had been broken so many times that the scars were part of the hardness of it.

I'm not saying I was perfect after accepting God into my life. I still made mistakes. I did stupid things that I regret, and I was disappointed by other Christians that I thought should be as perfect as their God was. It was all part of growing in the Lord. I stumbled, but I felt strong conviction that I—now a daughter of the King—was meant for better things than the depth to which I had allowed myself to fall.

Before having that sense of God-given purpose, I had been suffocating in my life and couldn't find any fresh air. I had been sinking and nearly drowning in a sea of bad decisions and desperation. Jesus not only threw me a lifeline, but He also gave me His secure and steady hand that pulled me up out of the mire. Where the emptiness of my life had only been superseded by my paralyzing fear, I now had Someone whose unconditional love was powerful enough to take away all fear and fill me with peace and joy. Jesus restored me and convinced me I had a purpose. And I knew it was good because *He* is good.

Recognize that You Have a Purpose

If you are a believer, you have a purpose. Don't ever think you don't. We can too easily become sidetracked about this because we watch too much television and think everything we read in a newspaper or magazine is true. Get this straight in your mind: The Bible is true. Whatever is based on the Bible and written by honest believers should also be true. Everything else is suspect. Don't base your sense of purpose on what the world thinks is valuable.

Purpose is what God has purposed for you to do. It is what you do purposefully for the Lord.

Your calling is what *God* calls you to do. *He* leads you into it. *He* reveals the gifts He has put in you and how *He* wants you to use them. Ask God to show you the gifts He has placed in you.

If you already have a strong sense of purpose and calling, be thankful because not everyone has that. Pray you never lose sight of it. Ask God to redefine the vision He has given you so that you can stay on the right path and not become sidetracked or diverted with unnecessary activity or distractions.

If you don't have a sense of purpose, or you have a vague sense that you do have a purpose but have no idea what it is, then ask yourself, "What am I good at?" Write down your answer. Make a list. If you don't know the answer to that question, then ask yourself, "What do I *like* to do?" "What do I *enjoy* doing?" "What kind of work *could* I do if I learned the skills I need?" "What kind of skills would I *like* to learn?"

"What do I *want* to do well?" If you are having trouble with the answers to these questions, ask someone you trust to help you make this list.

Don't expect to know all the details of your purpose and calling. Sometimes just knowing you *have* a purpose and calling is good enough to keep you going on the right path. Whenever you become confused or doubtful about this, go back to what you *do* know is your calling. Let me remind you that your life has purpose simply because you are God's child. You are called to be a disciple of Jesus and share the good news about life in Him. "God is faithful, by whom you were called into the fellowship of His Son, Jesus Christ our Lord" (1 Corinthians 1:9). You are also called to serve God and glorify Him by being His hand extended to others.

Your greatest purpose and calling on earth is to worship God. You were created for that. Worship will be your greatest purpose throughout eternity. One of the many wonderful things that happen as a result of worshipping God is He gives you revelation for your life. Praising Him will help you to fulfill your purpose. "God has called us to *peace*" (1 Corinthians 7:15, emphasis added). He has called us to *holiness* (1 Thessalonians 4:7, emphasis added). He has called us to *liberty* (Galatians 5:13, emphasis added). And He has called us to become more like Him every day (Romans 8:29). Pursuing those things will also keep us on the path toward fulfilling our purpose.

If you have *had* a strong sense of purpose in the *past,* but at this stage in your life you feel you may have lost it, keep in mind there are many things affecting that. If you have had health problems, relational disappointments, financial struggles, or you've been overworked to the point of exhaustion, stressed to the breaking point, or viciously attacked by the enemy, any one of those things can shake your confidence about yourself and your life. Don't let your circumstances dictate your sense of purpose. Your calling and purpose come from God, and He does not change His mind about that.

Submit Your Work to God

Knowing your purpose doesn't mean every job you do is fraught with deep significance. God uses the work we do to prepare us. Some jobs will humble us, give us more compassion for others, train us for what is ahead, or be a means to an end. A job may serve to simply provide the funds to stay alive, have a place to live, help your child be in a good school, enable you to care for others, or support you as you further your education. Each job prepares you for another in some way, so don't get down if you are in one of those preparatory, maturing, means-to-an-end kind of jobs.

If at all possible, it's important to find work you care about because you will do a better job at something you enjoy. Do you like to help others? In what ways do you like to help them? Do you like to teach? Serve? Make things for them? Help them do what they need to do? Help them get well? Ask God to show you the answers to these questions.

Whatever you do as your work, submit it to God for His glory. Ask Him to be in charge of it and bless it. When you do that, even the parts of what you are doing that are unpleasant to you will be bearable. "Whatever you do, do it heartily, as to the Lord and not to men, knowing that from the Lord you will receive the reward of the inheritance; for you serve the Lord Christ" (Colossians 3:23-24). You will always succeed at something you love and dedicate to God.

If you feel the work you have is not what you are supposed to be doing, ask God to move you out of that and into your real purpose. If your work situation is beating you down or making you sick, depressed, or anxious, or it just feels plain wrong to you, then ask God to give you a new vision for your life. You don't have to live adrift in your occupation—feeling aimless, inadequate, untalented, or purposeless. You can live a dynamic life of power and purpose no matter what work you are doing, if it is the will of God for your life.

Regardless of what you do, when your greatest motivation is to help others, it will be your greatest satisfaction as well (Philippians 2:4).

The Anointing of God

The Bible says, "The gifts and the calling of God are irrevocable" (Romans 11:29). God has placed gifts in you and He has a calling on your life, and that truth never changes. Whether you seek to recognize your gifts and understand your calling is up to you. God will not try to hide your calling from you. In fact, He often makes it so obvious that we don't even recognize it because we are looking for something different.

However, don't become confused and think that the gifts and calling of God are the same as the anointing. God's anointing is a special touch of God on our lives. When we are operating in our own gifts and calling, this touch of God will bring these gifts alive so they can be used powerfully for His glory and His purpose. The anointing is a special presence of the Holy Spirit that ignites your gifts and calling so that they bring life to other people and fulfill God's plan.

It is important to know that this anointing *can* be lost. It can be forfeited by our disobedience or sin. An example of this was Samson. He had a gift of strength. And his calling was to use it for the glory of God. His strength was represented by his long hair, and he was instructed to never cut it. When he was foolishly fooling around with Delilah, he told her the secret of his strength. She drugged him, and when he was asleep she had someone cut his hair. He awoke to see that the Philistines had captured him. He thought he was still strong and could break free, but "*he did not know that the Lord had departed from him*" (Judges 16:20, emphasis added). The Lord withdrew from Samson because of his disobedience.

In another example, King Saul disobeyed God and lost God's anointing to be king of his people. Saul rejected instructions from God, so God rejected him from being king (1 Samuel 15:16-23). "*The Spirit of the* Lord *departed from Saul,* and a distressing spirit from the Lord troubled him*" (1 Samuel 16:14, emphasis added). God gives us gifts and a calling to fulfill our purpose in life, and He does not take them back. However, the anointing of God is a gift so priceless that if we don't value it and we turn our back on God's ways, we will lose it.

The Bible says, "You have an anointing from the Holy One" (1 John 2:20). It also says, "The anointing which you have received from Him abides in you" (1 John 2:27). The anointing comes from God and lives in you. It is a work of the Holy Spirit in and through you that causes the things you do that are directed by God—in conjunction with His will and purpose for your life—to be illuminated to others. Desire the anointing of the Lord on what you do, but take care that you in no way disobey the Lord or compromise His Spirit in you. I pray "that you would walk worthy of God who calls you into His own kingdom and glory" (1 Thessalonians 2:12).

You will never find your purpose away from the God who created you for a purpose in the first place. Don't let your mind "be corrupted from the simplicity that is in Christ" (2 Corinthians 11:3). If life becomes overwhelming to you, it's because you are trying to live it in your own effort—to make things happen yourself. Look to the Lord in worship and prayer, and He will get you where you need to go. He will enable you to do what He has called you to do.

✦ Prayer Power ✦

Lord, You knew me before I was born. Thank You that You predestined me to be saved and conformed to the image of Jesus. Thank You that You have called me and prepared me to glorify You (Romans 8:29-30). Give me a clear sense of Your purpose in my life. Help me to understand what is the hope of my calling and the exceeding greatness of Your power to enable me to fulfill that purpose.

I pray everything I do will support Your plans and purposes for my life. Show me the gifts You have put in me and how I can best develop them and use them for Your pleasure. Enable me to stay strong in Your ways so that Your purpose can be realized in my life.

I commit my work to You. I pray I will always be in Your will in whatever I do, and that I will do it well. I pray that all I do is pleasing to You and to those for whom and with whom I am working. No job is too small or too great as long as it is what

You have called me to do. Establish the work of my hands for Your pleasure and Your glory (Psalm 90:17).

Help me to understand what is the hope of my calling (Ephesians 1:17-18). Enable me to "be steadfast, immovable, always abounding in the work of the Lord" that You have given me to do, knowing that my "labor is not in vain in the Lord"—as long as it is *from* You and *for* You (1 Corinthians 15:58). Help me to live every day with a deep sense of Your purpose in my life.

In Jesus' name I pray.

✢ WORD POWER ✢

We know that all things work together for good to those who love God, to those who are the called according to His purpose.

ROMANS 8:28

May He grant you according to your heart's desire, and fulfill all your purpose.

PSALM 20:4

I, therefore, the prisoner of the Lord, beseech you to walk worthy of the calling with which you were called.

EPHESIANS 4:1

We also pray always for you that our God would count you worthy of this calling, and fulfill all the good pleasure of His goodness and the work of faith with power.

2 THESSALONIANS 1:11

My beloved brethren, be steadfast, immovable, always abounding in the work of the Lord, knowing that your labor is not in vain in the Lord.

1 CORINTHIANS 15:58

⇁ 15 ⇐

BASK IN GOD'S LOVE

———◆———

God is love. And He loves you unconditionally.

You have to know this with certainty if you want to experience freedom, wholeness, and true success. That's because God's love is healing, fulfilling, liberating, edifying, rejuvenating, and calming. Without full acceptance of His love in our lives, we are always striving, worried, anxious, and uncertain. We are unable to find peace.

God's love is undying and everlasting; His love is always there for you. Nothing can separate you from the love of God (Romans 8:38-39). We are the ones who put up barriers to receiving it by our own doubts and fears.

Not fully believing God loves us can cause us to do things out of insecurity. God's love makes us feel secure in ways that human love cannot. God's love is unfailing; human love isn't. God's love is unconditional; human love often puts up hoops for us to jump through and standards to live up to—or down to, as the case may be. God's love is limitless and healing; human love can be healing too, but it has limits. That's because God is perfect and people are not. God's love is forgiving, keeping no record of wrongs. Human love is often exacting, keeping a list of injustices. And while human love can make us feel better about ourselves, God's love transforms us.

Many of us don't feel worthy of God's love. We think we have failed in so many ways that He must surely not love us so much anymore. Or we feel unlovable because of unloving things people have done to us in our past.

When we ask Jesus into our lives, the Holy Spirit of God is in our hearts. He is love and He is eternal. So we have eternal love in our hearts. Can it be, then, that the things you or I do out of a pure heart filled with God's love will have an eternal aspect attached to them? Is that part of laying up treasures in heaven? (Matthew 6:19-20). "Where your treasure is, there your heart will be also" (Matthew 6:21). If so, then we can't afford to not be a *receiver of,* and a *channel for,* the love of God in this world.

If you doubt God loves you, go before Him and ask Him to help you sense His presence and His love. In order to heal, be made whole, and become enriched in your spirit and soul, you must do this often until it becomes part of you and is no longer something you have to grapple with. Going before God in worship and prayer, and thanking Him that He is the God of love, is the most wonderful, healing experience. Every time you do that, He will pour His love into you and it will grow. It doesn't get any better than that.

Don't just receive the idea that God loves you in your mind. Get it into your heart. Say, "Jesus loves me, this I know" 50 times a day, if necessary, until you become convinced. Invite God's presence—which is the presence of pure, unconditional love—with your praise. When you feel discouraged, go before God and thank Him for His love. Thank Him that He died for you, and now you will live forever with Him. If that isn't love, I don't know what is.

How God's Love Changes Your Life

God's love gives you everlasting life. "God so loved the world that He gave His only begotten Son, that whoever believes in Him should not perish but have everlasting life" (John 3:16).

God's love draws you to Him. "I drew them with gentle cords, with bands of love, and I was to them as those who take the yoke from their neck. I stooped and fed them" (Hosea 11:4).

God's love lets you live through Him. "In this the love of God was manifested toward us, that God has sent His only begotten Son into the world, that we might live through Him" (1 John 4:9).

God's love paid for your sins. "In this is love, not that we loved God, but that He loved us and sent His Son to be the propitiation for our sins" (1 John 4:10).

God's love gives you access to Him. "We have known and believed the love that God has for us. God is love, and he who abides in love abides in God, and God in him" (1 John 4:16).

God's love frees you from fear. "There is no fear in love; but perfect love casts out fear, because fear involves torment. But he who fears has not been made perfect in love" (1 John 4:18).

God's love gives you true success. "In all these things we are more than conquerors through Him who loved us" (Romans 8:37).

Receiving God's love frees you from having to exact love from others. God's love allows you to not keep score about how loving they are, or if they are meeting your need for love or not. The love of God is not just a feeling you have. It is God's presence within you and around you. No matter what your concept of God's love is, it is so much greater than you think. And you will spend a lifetime trying to comprehend it.

God's Love Frees You to Love Others

The more you receive the love of God, the more it flows through you to others. In fact, our love for other people is the most compelling sign of all to an unbeliever. It was the love of God I saw in other people that drew me toward the Lord. It is the love of God in me that has filled me with love for others—even people in other places whom I don't know.

Jesus said, "A new commandment I give to you, that you love one another; as I have loved you" (John 13:34). Jesus loved us so much that He laid down His life for us. We don't have to die for others, but we can lay down our life in other ways.

The Bible says that if we don't have love in our heart for others, we have nothing and whatever good we think we do, we will not benefit from it. "Though I speak with the tongues of men and of angels, but have not love, I have become sounding brass or a clanging cymbal... and though I have all faith, so that I could remove mountains, but have not love, I am nothing" (1 Corinthians 13:1-2). God wants to fill your heart with His love so that you can extend it to others.

TWELVE WAYS TO EXTEND
GOD'S LOVE TO OTHERS

There are countless ways to extend God's love to others, but here are just a few found in Romans 12:9-21, a passage of Scripture that could also be titled "How to Act Like a Christian."

1. *"Let love be without hypocrisy" (verse 9).* Do not pretend to love others when you actually don't. If you have no love in your heart for someone, pray for them every day and God will give you His heart of love for them. Don't just *say* you love someone, *show* it. Do and say things that can be defined as acts of love. Ask God to fill your heart with His love and show you how to share it.

2. *"Abhor what is evil" (verse 9).* You are a person who is already sensitive to evil or you wouldn't even be reading this book. But our society has become so filled with evil that we can become numb to some of the "tamer stuff," and so it no longer offends us as it should. Ask God to show you if that is happening to you. Say, "Holy Spirit, help me to be grieved by everything that

grieves You. Help me to detest any acts or words that are unloving or sinful." When you do this, you not only show your love for God; you also show your love for others. That's because when you have godly standards, others feel safe around you.

3. *"Cling to what is good" (verse 9)*. It is not enough to be repulsed by evil; we must actively cling to the Lord and all that is good. Good is everything that is motivated by God's love. Cling to the love of God in your heart and let it be the guide for all you do.

4. *"Be kindly affectionate to one another with brotherly love, in honor giving preference to one another" (verse 10)*. Being kind and affectionate to others—loving them the way you would a beloved brother or sister—manifests by honoring them and putting their needs before your own. Pray, "Lord, help me to take someone else's needs into consideration before my own." Showing love means not being indifferent toward others.

5. *"Not lagging in diligence" (verse 11)*. This means being diligent in all we do—not just being diligent sometimes, when we feel like it, or when we want to. It means loving others all the time.

6. *"Fervent in spirit" (verse 11)*. Being fervent in spirit also means being fervent in prayer. It's being passionate about the things God cares about. It means fervently loving others and passionately loving God.

7. *"Serving the Lord" (verse 11)*. Think of everything you do as service to God—and that includes loving others. Believe that because you love God so much, you will do anything for Him and everything to please Him—even loving the unlovable.

8. *"Continuing steadfastly in prayer" (verse 12)*. Praying all the time about everything is the way to live a praying life. One of the most important things we pray about is other people and their needs. That is one of the most loving things to do.

9. *"Distributing to the needs of the saints, given to hospitality" (verse*

13). Ask God to show you the needs of others. Of course, you can't meet every need of every person, but *God* can. Show the love of God by giving in any way you can—as the Holy Spirit leads—to meet the needs of people around you.

10. *"Rejoice with those who rejoice" (verse 15).* Even when everything is going wrong in *your* life, and you see people rejoicing over things *you* have been longing for, rejoice *with* them. Resist any tendency to feel envy. That is the opposite of love.

11. *"Weep with those who weep" (verse 15).* There are so many people hurting right now who would be blessed by your love and compassion. They need you to show empathy and weep with them. That show of love can change someone's life.

12. *"If it is possible, as much as depends on you, live peaceably with all men" (verse 18).* Do all you can to avoid being offensive, difficult, divisive, or contentious with others. Ask God to help you always be peaceful, cooperative, agreeable, and pleasant.

Faith, hope, and love are lasting. But the greatest of these is love (1 Corinthians 13:13). That's because God is love and He is eternal. When we go to be with the Lord, we won't need faith and hope anymore, because we will see Him face-to-face. But we will bask in the love of God forever.

⤳ Prayer Power ⤶

Lord, I thank You that You are the God of love. Thank You for loving me even before I knew You (Romans 5:8). Thank You for sending Your Son, Jesus, to die for me and take on Himself all I deserve. Thank You, Jesus, that You have given me life with You forever, and a better life now. Your love heals me and makes me whole. "You are my Lord, my goodness is nothing apart from You" (Psalm 16:2).

I know there is a great dimension of healing and wholeness that can only happen in the presence of Your love. Enable me to open up to Your love working in my life as never before. Wash over me with Your love today. Fill my heart with Your love in greater measure so that I can be the whole person You created me to be.

Perfect Your love in me by helping me to love other people the way that *You* love them. Give me Your heart of love for others at all times. I pray I will be so filled with Your love that it overflows to other people in a way that they can perceive it. Show me the loving thing to do in every situation.

How grateful I am that nothing can separate me from Your love, no matter where I go or what I do—not even my own failings (Romans 8:35-39). Thank You that because of Your love for me, I am more than a conqueror (Romans 8:37). Thank You, Lord, that Your unfailing love and mercy surround me because I trust in You (Psalm 32:10).

In Jesus' name I pray.

✣ WORD POWER ✣

I am persuaded that neither death nor life, nor angels
nor principalities nor powers, nor things present
nor things to come, nor height nor depth, nor any
other created thing, shall be able to separate us from
the love of God which is in Christ Jesus our Lord.

ROMANS 8:38-39

Who shall separate us from the love of Christ?
Shall tribulation, or distress, or persecution, or
famine, or nakedness, or peril, or sword?

ROMANS 8:35

God, who is rich in mercy, because of His great
love with which He loved us, even when we
were dead in trespasses, made us alive together
with Christ (by grace you have been saved), and
raised us up together, and made us sit together
in the heavenly places in Christ Jesus.

EPHESIANS 2:4-6

Beloved, let us love one another, for love is of God; and
everyone who loves is born of God and knows God. He
who does not love does not know God, for God is love.

1 JOHN 4:7-8

You shall love the LORD your God with all your
heart, with all your soul, and with all your mind.

MATTHEW 22:37

❖ 16 ❖

PUT YOUR HOPE
IN THE LORD

———◈◈◈———

I used to think hope was something that just happened to people, like getting blue eyes or brown eyes in the gene pool. Or winning the lottery. Some people have it and some people don't. I didn't have it. I pretended I did for as long as I could pull it off, but nothing ever worked out. So I transferred any hope I had over to luck because the odds seemed better. But that didn't work, either. My luck ran out very early on. I knew I was at the end of trying to figure things out on my own, and I had no one else to rely on. When I think back to the hopelessness I felt just before I became a believer, it's a wonder I lived through it. Someone must have been praying for me.

After I became a believer, I knew my life no longer depended on luck. But I still felt hopeless about a lot of things—such as ever marrying a godly and faithful man, ever amounting to anything, or ever doing something of any significance. It wasn't until I read about hope in the Bible that I discovered hope is a decision we make. *We* decide whether to have hope or not. *We* make the call as to whether we will give place to hopelessness. *We* are the ones who acknowledge that hope is within us in the form of the Holy Spirit.

Paul prayed that the God of hope would fill believers with joy and peace so that they could "abound in hope by the power of the Holy Spirit" (Romans 15:13). He also said that because the Holy Spirit has filled our hearts with the love of God, we would never be disappointed by putting our hope in Him (Romans 5:5). That means we *always* have hope, because the Holy Spirit *in* us is a guarantee that we have access to the God of the impossible. We can *choose* to have hope, no matter what is happening in our life, because our expectations are in Him.

How to Avoid Suffering from Hope-Deferred Syndrome

Hope means you anticipate something good happening. But when time goes on and it seems as though what you hoped for will never happen, that can make your heart hurt. "Hope deferred makes the heart sick, but when the desire comes, it is a tree of life" (Proverbs 13:12). We can't live with a chronically hurting heart. We need the tree of life. When we are mired down in hopelessness, disappointment, and heartache, we can't live in the freedom, wholeness, and true success God has for us. A broken heart paves the way for a broken life—a life that is not working.

Believe in God

The first thing we have to do to avoid hopelessness is to make a decision to believe God. We have to tell ourselves to put our hope in the Lord. We have to require it of ourselves. We have to choose to trust in God. This is especially true when we hope to see changes in other people. We pray and pray, but they still exert their own will by refusing to hear God speaking to their heart. We must force ourselves to take our eyes off that person and situation and put them on the Lord. We have to put our hope in Him and know He is in charge. That doesn't mean we stop praying. It means that every time we pray, we trust that God hears and will answer in His way and in His time.

I know this is hard, but it is the only way to have peace in your life. Your happiness cannot depend on someone else, even if you are married. It depends on God. Your hope and expectations must be in *Him.*

Hope means to desire something with the expectation of attaining it. When we put our hope in the Lord, we have an expectation that He will come through for us. "If we hope for what we do not see, we eagerly wait for it with perseverance" (Romans 8:25). We can persevere in hope because we believe God.

Paul told the Hebrews about "this hope we have as an anchor of the soul, both sure and steadfast" (Hebrews 6:19). We can't have that sense of our soul being anchored—especially when we are in the midst of a storm—if we don't have our hope in the Lord. He also says we should be "rejoicing in hope" (Romans 12:12). To rejoice in hope is a decision we make in the face of unanswered prayer. Because let's face it, we can become hopeless when our prayers are not answered.

Read God's Word

The second thing we have to do to avoid hopelessness is to read God's Word. "Whatever things were written before were written for our learning, that we through the patience and comfort of the Scriptures might have hope" (Romans 15:4). If we don't have hope in our heart, then we are listening to lies from the enemy, looking at our circumstances, or trusting our fears and doubts. We need the truth from God to deflect those things. Because one of the purposes of the Bible is to bring us hope, we must deliberately say, "Lord, I put my hope in Your Word" (Psalm 119:81).

Peter said to "sanctify the Lord God in your hearts, and always be ready to give a defense to everyone who asks you a reason for the hope that is in you, with meekness and fear" (1 Peter 3:15). We cannot give a reason for the hope in us if we feel hopeless. If we feel hopeless, then our hope is not in the Lord or His Word. People who are happy are those who put their hope in Him—even in the face of unanswered prayer (Psalm 146:5).

Hope Is Not a Small Thing

Sometimes the small things determine how something will work out in our lives. God wants us to be diligent in the small things as well as in the large. This is a reflection of character as far as God is concerned. "He who is faithful in what is least is faithful also in much; and he who is unjust in what is least is unjust also in much" (Luke 16:10). The little things can ruin everything. People often concern themselves only with the big things and let the little ones slide, but God sees them all as important. It may seem like a small thing to allow yourself to feel hopeless, but it can quickly turn into a big thing. Hope is a very big thing in your life, and it adds to your true success more than you might think. Don't leave home without it. In fact, don't *stay* home without it, either.

Put Your Hope in God and Not in Your Own Strength

God chooses the weak and small to confound the strong (1 Corinthians 1:27). We all have weaknesses, but the Lord says your weakness can be your ultimate strength. That's because He wants to show Himself strong in your weakness and use it for His glory. The reason He does this is because He does not like *our* taking credit for what *He* does. He uses our weakness for His purpose so that we know it is *Him* doing it and not ourselves.

When it comes to your own weaknesses, submit them to God. Tell Him you know it is *His* power working in you that will make things happen. Look at your own weakness as a blessing, because God can do something great through you. And that gives you good reason to hope.

God is your hope. If you hope in your talent, abilities, or efforts, you have no way to rise above your own limitations. But when your hope is in the God of the impossible, then anything is possible in your life—even accomplishing things beyond your own ability.

When you feel hopeless about anything in your life, ask God to reignite your hope in Him and His ability to do the impossible. When you have hope in the Lord, you will have joy in your heart. "The hope of the righteous will be gladness" (Proverbs 10:28).

Wherever God is enthroned, the enemy cannot win. Wherever God is enthroned, hope rules.

✧ PRAYER POWER ✦

Lord, I depend entirely on You. In You I put all my hope and expectations. No matter what happens, "I will hope continually, and will praise You yet more and more" (Psalm 71:14). Help me to become a prisoner of hope (Zechariah 9:12). I know that I have no hope without You, Lord (Ephesians 2:12), so my hope is entirely in You (Psalm 39:7). "For You are my hope, O Lord GOD; You are my trust from my youth" (Psalm 71:5).

In the times I am tempted to feel hopeless—especially when I don't see answers to my prayers for a long time and I become discouraged—help me to put my eyes back on You. Enable me to end all feelings of hopelessness in my life. Help me to see they are not true and that only Your Word is true. When I pray for a person or a situation and I don't see changes, help me to not put my hope in answered prayer, but rather to put my hope in You, the One who answers my prayers. Where I have put my hope and expectations on people or circumstances, I confess that as a lack of faith in You and Your Word. Help me to stop doing that and start putting my hope and expectations in You.

I take comfort in Your Word and Your promises. In Your presence is where my heart has found a home. I trust in You—the God of hope—who has given me every reason to hope. Help me to see that having hope is a big issue and that it is a clear indicator of the condition of my heart. Teach me to always refuse hopelessness and choose to hope in You.

In Jesus' name I pray.

✧ WORD POWER ✦

Behold, the eye of the LORD is on those who
fear Him, on those who hope in His mercy.

PSALM 33:18

Hope does not disappoint, because the love
of God has been poured out in our hearts
by the Holy Spirit who was given to us.

ROMANS 5:5

O Israel, hope in the LORD; for with the LORD there
is mercy, and with Him is abundant redemption.

PSALM 130:7

Happy is he who has the God of Jacob for his
help, whose hope is in the LORD his God.

PSALM 146:5

May the God of hope fill you with all joy and
peace in believing, that you may abound in
hope by the power of the Holy Spirit.

ROMANS 15:13

GIVE GOD'S WAY— TO HIM AND TO OTHERS

Giving is a big part of having true success in life. I believe it is a natural law that "the generous soul will be made rich, and he who waters will also be watered himself" (Proverbs 11:25). I have seen that proven true among believers and nonbelievers alike. When people give, something is open and operational in their lives, and blessings are released to them. But it's even more so for a believer.

When Jesus was teaching believers how to live, He said, "Give, and it will be given to you: good measure, pressed down, shaken together, and running over will be put into your bosom. For with the same measure that you use, it will be measured back to you" (Luke 6:38). The guarantee here is that when believers give, it comes back to them measure for measure.

There are two ways to give. One is to give to God. The other is to give to those in need as *if* you are giving to God.

Giving to God Because He Gives So Much to You

Having grown up poor, I was always afraid of not having enough food or a safe place to live. As a result, I started working as soon as I could. I began babysitting when I was 12 years old, and then I obtained a real job when I was 16. From that point on I always had at least one job and sometimes two—even when I was going to college full time.

When I received the Lord and started attending church, I put money in the collection plate according to what I had with me. As I grew more in the Word, I came to see that giving to God is really *giving back* to God from what He had given to me. It was a step of obedience to Him—a way to please Him. God asks us to try Him and see if He is not faithful to pour out blessings upon us and to give us everything we need (Malachi 3:10).

It was a hard step to learn to give to God until I got over being afraid of being homeless and starving to death. It really comes down to how much we trust God to provide for us.

When Jesus said to "seek first the kingdom of God and His righteousness, and all these things will be added to you," He was talking about food, clothing, and money (Matthew 6:25-34). He was saying not to worry about these things, but instead to seek God and His ways. One of His ways is giving. If we rob God of what He wants from us, we are robbing ourselves of all He wants to give us (Malachi 3:8-11).

I'm not just talking about money here, but let's start with that. God has requirements for us with regard to money that we need to adhere to when we give to Him. And whenever we give to God for the furthering of His kingdom on earth, something is released to us. It's as if a giant storehouse up in heaven is opened up and riches are poured out on our lives. Actually, God opens the "windows of heaven" and He pours out such blessings on us that "there will not be room enough to receive it" (Malachi 3:10).

When we give to God, He will not allow the devourer to destroy our lives (Malachi 3:11). It may not be that a block of solid gold or a pack of one-hundred-dollar bills will fall down on our head, but it might be that we don't get sick, things don't break down, we find a place to live for a good price, or we are offered a better job. Whatever we give to God, it all adds up to a better life for us here on earth. Remember that all God's laws are for our benefit. Giving a tithe of what we have to God is for His purpose, but it turns out to be for our benefit as well.

Giving to God makes Him happy, and He wants *us* to be happy doing it. He wants us to give for the joy of giving (Matthew 6:1-4). His Word says, "He who sows sparingly will also reap sparingly, and he who sows bountifully will also reap bountifully. So let each one give as he purposes in his heart, not grudgingly or of necessity; for God loves a cheerful giver" (2 Corinthians 9:6-7). He wants us to give liberally and have a good attitude about it. When we do, He will do the same for us.

Ask God to help you give to Him the way He wants you to. Ask Him to guide you in this step of obedience. It's an important part of being able to receive all He has for you.

Giving to Others in Need

Our happiness is related to our own generosity. "He who has a generous eye will be blessed, for he gives of his bread to the poor" (Proverbs 22:9). People who have a generous eye look out for others in need. They watch to see who they can help and how they can do it. And in the process, God rewards them.

Jesus is the light of the world. When we receive Him, His light lives in us and shines through us. Others see that light in us and are drawn to it, even though they might not know what it is. "It is the God who commanded light to shine out of darkness, who has shone in our hearts to give the light of the knowledge of the glory of God in the face of Jesus Christ" (2 Corinthians 4:6).

When we don't give to others, we don't allow the light of the Lord to be fully revealed in us. We cover it as if we are slanting the blinds to restrict the light. The light is still there; it just can't be seen as brightly. But we can ask God to help us give so that His light will shine through us to others.

We must not be reluctant to give. With regard to the poor, the Bible says, "You shall surely give to him, and your heart should not be grieved when you give to him, because for this thing the LORD your God will bless you in all your works and in all to which you put your hand" (Deuteronomy 15:10). God blesses our work when we give to those in need. With regard to the giver, the Bible says, "There is one who scatters, yet increases more; and there is one who withholds more than is right, but it leads to poverty" (Proverbs 11:24). We increase when we give; we decrease when we don't give.

Giving is not just about money. It's about giving whatever is needed. If you don't have money, you can give your time to drive someone where they want to go, take them something they need, or do something for them they can't do well themselves. There are many ways to meet the needs of others if you just ask God to show you. Give to other people without expecting anything back from them. Keep the focus on giving to please God.

I have found that when I need breakthrough or release in my life, I check to see if there are ways I should be giving to others. Perhaps I have something they need or there is something I can do or say that would help them or be an encouragement. Don't ever feel you have nothing to give, because that is never true. You have the Lord, who is the source of your supply. One of the greatest gifts someone ever gave me was a promise to pray for me. That was more valuable to me than anything. I have also given that same gift to others. And I have found that even those who don't know the Lord are still surprisingly happy to receive prayer.

There is so much you can give to others. Ask God to show you. Say, "Lord, who do I need to give something to today? Show me what I should give." The more you give, as the Lord leads, the more that releases the flow of all God has for you.

✣ Prayer Power ✦

Lord, teach me how to give to You with a cheerful attitude. Help me to be diligent in this step of obedience. I don't ever want to rob You; I want only to bless You. Help me to give to You as You require. Teach my heart to release back to You from all You have given to me. Help me to reject the fear of not having enough. When I become fearful, help me to put my trust in You. You are greater than any lack I may face.

Help me to have a "generous soul" and a "generous eye" (Proverbs 11:25; 22:9). Show me specific ways I can give to others. Reveal their needs and how I can meet them. Show me what You want me to give and to whom. I want to be led by Your Spirit and know that what I give is pleasing to You. I know You bless the person who gives to You and who gives to those in need. I don't want to stop up the flow of Your blessings in my life by not giving when I should. I am grateful for all You have given me, but I pray I will not merely give to get, but give only to please You.

Help me to understand the release that happens in my life when I give so that I can let go of things. Help me to "not forget to do good and to share," for I know that with such sacrifices, You are "well pleased" (Hebrews 13:16). Help me to give and thereby store up treasures in heaven that do not fail, for I know that where my treasure is, my heart will be there also (Luke 12:33-34).

In Jesus' name I pray.

⇢ WORD POWER ⇠

Blessed is he who considers the poor; the LORD will deliver him in time of trouble. The LORD will preserve him and keep him alive, and he will be blessed on the earth; You will not deliver him to the will of his enemies. The LORD will strengthen him on his bed of illness; You will sustain him on his sickbed.

PSALM 41:1-3

The generous soul will be made rich, and he who waters will also be watered himself.

PROVERBS 11:25

"Bring all the tithes into the storehouse, that there
may be food in My house, and try Me now in this,"
says the Lord of hosts, "if I will not open for you the
windows of heaven and pour out for you such blessing
that there will not be room enough to receive it."

MALACHI 3:10

Jesus said to him, "If you want to be perfect, go, sell
what you have and give to the poor, and you will
have treasure in heaven; and come, follow Me."

MATTHEW 19:21

Command those who are rich in this present age
not to be haughty, nor to trust in uncertain riches
but in the living God, who gives us richly all things
to enjoy. Let them do good, that they be rich in
good works, ready to give, willing to share, storing
up for themselves a good foundation for the time
to come, that they may lay hold on eternal life.

1 TIMOTHY 6:17-19

→ 18 ←

TAKE CONTROL OF
YOUR THOUGHTS

———

I used to think my thoughts were something that just happened to me, as if they flew into my mind like birds into a tree and I could not control them. It wasn't until I received the Lord and saw what the Bible teaches on the subject that I realized we can *take charge* of our thoughts. In fact, we are instructed to do so.

You may not be able to control every thought that flies into your mind, but you *can* control how long it perches there. You can decide whether that thought is just passing through or it's nesting. Your thoughts affect your entire life. That's why you must take charge of them and not allow any birdbrained ideas to control you.

Thoughts falling under that category can be tormenting. *I always fail at everything I do. I know I'll fail at this too.* They can be based on lies. *No one loves me. Even God doesn't love me.* They can cause bitterness. *I still resent what that person did to me. I wish they would suffer the way they made me suffer.* They can be immoral. *I know that person is married, but I can't stop thinking about him (her) all the time.* Or they can be downright evil. *I could have an affair with that person and my husband (wife) would never have to know.*

The definition of birdbrained thoughts is "annoyingly stupid and shallow," and believe me, that is exactly the way we see these kinds of thoughts when we become free of them. We allow thoughts like these to overtake us because of our own lack of wholeness. The brokenness of our soul can create the perfect environment in which they can thrive. When we become free, those thoughts are no longer welcome.

The enemy of your soul will do whatever it takes to get inside your mind with his lies. He will plant a thought, a fear, a suspicion, or a wrong idea and torment you with it. It is meant to wear you down. And it works. We must learn to recognize his deception before we can refute and resist it.

The only way to fight his lies is with the truth of the Word. "The night is far spent, the day is at hand. Therefore let us cast off the works of darkness, and let us put on the armor of light" (Romans 13:12). We can put on the armor of light by speaking the Word of God out loud. We can pray out loud using Scripture in our prayers. And we can speak and sing words of worship and praise to the Lord.

It is a dangerous thing to just let our thoughts go wherever they take us. "I have stretched out My hands all day long to a rebellious people, who walk in a way that is not good, according to their own thoughts" (Isaiah 65:2). We don't want to be rebellious against God by going wherever our thoughts take us. We have control over them. We can ask ourselves, *What am I letting into my mind? What is the fruit of the thoughts I am thinking? Do my thoughts produce positive and uplifting results? Or do they make me feel bad, sad, anxious, fearful, depressed, or angry? Are these thoughts from the Lord? Or do they seem more like something that comes from the enemy?* When you have God's Word in your mind, you will recognize anything that does not line up with it.

You Can Always Change Your Mind

Paul said to the Corinthians, "I fear, lest somehow, as the serpent deceived Eve by his craftiness, so your minds may be corrupted from the simplicity that is in Christ" (2 Corinthians 11:3). When things start becoming confusing or vague—or your mind is anxious, fearful, doubt filled, stressed, or overwhelmed—that is not from the Lord. It never is. The simplicity in Christ is crystal clear, positive, peaceful, faith filled, and calm. Don't settle for anything less. "God is not the author of confusion but of peace" (1 Corinthians 14:33).

Your mind can be renewed. Paul said to the Ephesians, "Put off, concerning your former conduct, the old man which grows corrupt according to the deceitful lusts, and be renewed in the spirit of your mind" (Ephesians 4:22-23). *We* can decide to put off wrong ways of thinking or acting—the old self that attracts deception and lust like a magnet—and deliberately be renewed in our mind. We can "put on the new man which was created according to God, in true righteousness and holiness" (Ephesians 4:24). We can reject any other spirit in our mind that is not the Holy Spirit.

So, contrary to what I used to believe, when our thoughts start flying south, we can stop the migration and cry foul. (Sorry!) We have to say, "No, this is not happening on my watch." And the reason we can do that is because we have the Holy Spirit in us. We can put the Holy Spirit in charge of our mind. We can refuse the spirit of depression or doubt. We can reject the spirit of fear. Those thoughts come from the enemy of our soul.

The more you know God—by reading His Word and spending time with Him in prayer and worship—the more you can discern what thoughts are of Him and what thoughts are either from your flesh or the enemy. For example, if you find yourself thinking a thought such as, *I would be better off dead,* you will be able to recognize that this is not God giving you revelation for your life.

This doesn't mean that you deny having undesirable or wrong thoughts. Nor should you push them down and repress them. It requires examining what is going on in your mind in the light of Scripture to see if your thoughts line up with what God says in His Word.

We all have to become good at resisting wrong thoughts. I am a target of the enemy attack on my mind just as much as anyone else. With every single book I have written—more than 50 now—the enemy has come to me and said, "You can't do this." "You'll never finish it." "This is the last book you'll ever write." In the beginning I used to put up with those thoughts for a while before I figured out what was going on. Then I started recognizing the same pattern. Now, when those thoughts of doubt come over me, I say, "It's true. I can't write this book. There is no way I can finish it. And this will be the last book I ever write if I turn my back on God. But that's not going to happen. I depend entirely on the Lord to help me write this book. And whether I ever write another one is entirely up to Him. But I have the mind of Christ, and I can do all things through Christ who strengthens me. Thanks for reminding me. And now I'm telling my heavenly Father on you."

Then I go before God and say, "Lord, I thank You that You have given me authority over all the power of the enemy. I rebuke the plans of the enemy to torment me with the thoughts of fear, failure, doubt, and depression. Thank You that You have given me the mind of Christ. I fully realize that by myself I cannot write this book. I depend on You to inspire me, lead me, give me revelation, and enable me to do beyond what I can do on my own. I give this book to You and ask You to speak through me so that it accomplishes the purpose You have for it."

The truth is, your thoughts will either serve your flesh or the enemy or the Lord. And the decision is yours. Paul said that evil caused his flesh to war against his mind. He asked who would deliver him from this, and then he answered his own question, saying, "I thank God—through Jesus Christ our Lord! So then, with the mind I myself serve the law of God, but with the flesh the law of sin" (Romans 7:25). Jesus is the Deliverer who sets us free from our own ungodly thoughts.

Because of Jesus, you can change your mind!

Glorify God in Your Mind

The carnal mind is controlled by our flesh. It is an enemy of God because it does not want to obey Him. If we are in the flesh—letting our fleshly thoughts be in charge of our mind—we "cannot please God" (Romans 8:8). Believe me, you don't want to be living in a way that does not please God. That will shut out the blessings He has for you, and delay what He has planned for your life.

Our fleshly thoughts will keep us from glorifying God. "Although they knew God, they did not glorify Him as God, nor were thankful, but became futile in their thoughts, and their foolish hearts were darkened" (Romans 1:21). The only sure remedy for that is to worship God, because worship will always flood your mind and heart with light. Praise Jesus that because of Him, and by the power of the Holy Spirit, you can be set free from ungodly thoughts that not only damage the soul but hinder all God has for you.

No matter how strong you are in the Lord, the enemy will always attempt to get you to believe a lie. Lying is the only way he gains power over anyone. The enemy will come to tell you that "You are a failure," "There is no way out," "Things will never change," "You will always feel this way," "God doesn't care about you," and on and on. Don't accept as truth the lies the enemy feeds you. Ask yourself, "Are my thoughts contrary to God's Word?" Sin begins with a thought in the mind (Mark 7:21-22). People don't *fall* into an adulterous relationship. It begins in the mind first. And that's the place to put a stop to it. When you have tormenting thoughts, or thoughts you know are not of the Lord, do what the Bible says and think only about things that are *true, noble, just, pure, lovely, of good report, virtuous,* or *praiseworthy* (Philippians 4:8, emphasis added). Ask God to help you cast down "every high thing that exalts itself against the knowledge of God" and to bring "every thought into captivity to the obedience of Christ" (2 Corinthians 10:5).

Freedom, wholeness, and true success cannot be achieved unless the thoughts in your mind line up with the truth of God's Word.

⤳ PRAYER POWER ⤺

Lord, help me to cast down every thought I have that is not glorifying to You. Enable me to bring my thoughts into captivity and obedience to You and Your ways. I know it is "You who test the righteous, and see the mind and heart" (Jeremiah 20:12). Show me what is in my mind and heart that is not pleasing to You. Reveal to me any lies of the enemy that I have accepted as truth. "Examine me, O LORD, and prove me; try my mind and my heart" (Psalm 26:2). Help me to live with the love, power, and sound mind You have given me.

Teach me the truth of Your Word so well that I recognize a lie the moment it presents itself. I know I cannot move into all You have for me if I believe lies about myself, my circumstances, or You. Help me to silence the voice of the enemy by speaking Your truth. Give me clarity of thought to replace any confusion. I pray that Your Word will discern my "thoughts and intents of the heart" whenever I read it (Hebrews 4:12).

Enable me to choose this day to fill my mind with "the best, not the worst; the beautiful, not the ugly; things to praise, not things to curse" (Philippians 4:8 MSG). Help me to think straight and not daydream or fantasize. Help me to not entertain thoughts of unforgiveness against anyone or dwell on what has happened in the past. I pray that Your peace, which surpasses all understanding, will guard my heart and mind through Jesus, my Lord (Philippians 4:7).

In Jesus' name I pray.

✣ WORD POWER ✦

Do not be conformed to this world, but be
transformed by the renewing of your mind,
that you may prove what is that good and
acceptable and perfect will of God.

ROMANS 12:2

You will keep him in perfect peace, whose mind
is stayed on You, because he trusts in You.

ISAIAH 26:3

You should no longer walk as the rest of the Gentiles
walk, in the futility of their mind, having their

understanding darkened, being alienated from
the life of God, because of the ignorance that is
in them, because of the blindness of their heart.

EPHESIANS 4:17-18

To be carnally minded is death, but to be
spiritually minded is life and peace.

ROMANS 8:6

Let this mind be in you which was also in Christ Jesus.

PHILIPPIANS 2:5

19

REFUSE NEGATIVE EMOTIONS

God cares about your feelings and emotions. He doesn't want you to be ruled by them. The Bible says of God that "He heals the brokenhearted and binds up their wounds" (Psalm 147:3). He doesn't want you to just find a way to cope with negative emotions that undermine your life. He wants you to be completely free of them so you can become the whole person He made you to be.

When we are emotionally fragile and hurting, we are not whole. Being whole means having peace about who you are and what you are doing. It means coming to a place of peace about your past and realizing you don't have to live there anymore. That takes recognizing and embracing the good aspects of it and coming to terms with the troubling, disappointing, or hurtful parts of it. Wholeness also means having peace about your present situation—even if you feel it is not yet good—because you trust that God will make it right. It also means having peace about your future, no matter how scary it may seem. It is trusting that because you have surrendered your life to the Lord, your future is safe in His hands. You have confidence that you are aligned with God's will and purpose for your life, and you have an inner joy because of that knowledge. When you can maintain such peace, then you will no longer struggle with negative emotions and you find the freedom, wholeness, and true success you want.

Why Do I Still Hurt?

The amount of hurt and brokenness you experienced in your past will determine how much healing you need now in order to be whole. No matter what horrible things you have been through, how young you were when they happened, how old you are now, or how much of your life was spent living the wrong way in reaction to it, you can still be set free from negative emotions. That kind of freedom cannot be found outside of God's love. He is the only one with the power to do a complete work of emotional healing in you.

You must know, first of all, that you don't have to live with chronic emotional pain or negative emotions. You don't have to hurt all the time. The reason I know this is because I lived with these feelings every day of my life for more than 30 years. I remember feeling depressed, anxious, fearful, hurting, hopeless, unloved, rejected, and distraught for as far back as I can remember. But one by one, God set me free from all that. Do I ever feel any of these emotions anymore? Yes, some of them, but not all. I don't feel rejected or unloved anymore because I am accepted and loved by God. I can feel depressed when depressing things happen, and anxious or fearful about scary things that happen around me, but I don't live there. I take those feelings to God, and He sets me free from them.

If I can get free of negative emotions, you can too. It is never too late to be liberated. Being set free doesn't mean you will never have another problem or that you will never feel fearful, depressed, or anxious again. But when upsetting things happen, these things do not control your life.

In order to get free of negative emotions, you have to take charge and say, "I am not going to live my life in pain and brokenness. God has given me a way out, and I am going to take it. I am determined to stop all wrong thinking." Achieving freedom from emotional pain happens as you take a step at a time with the Lord and He helps you to change habits of thought, feeling, and action.

The balm of Gilead mentioned in the Bible was a substance known in that area at the time for its healing qualities. The prophet Jeremiah asked God, "Is there no balm in Gilead? Is there no physician there? Why then is there no healing for the wound of my people?" (Jeremiah 8:22 NIV).

We often ask God the same question. "Why do I still hurt, God?" "Why can't I get free?" "How much longer must I live with depression and sadness?" "Why can't I get rid of this horrible fear and anxiety?" "Why have You not healed me?"

Sometimes the answer to those questions can be the same as what God told Jeremiah. He answered Jeremiah saying, "'They go from one sin to another; they do not acknowledge me,' declares the LORD" (Jeremiah 9:3 NIV).

When you allow any sin a place in your heart, you are not obeying God. And you won't be able to find the freedom, healing, and restoration you desire. It's there for you, but you have to do your part and confess all sin and acknowledge your dependence on God for everything. "O my soul, you have said to the LORD, 'You are my Lord, my goodness is nothing apart from You'" (Psalm 16:2).

How Do I Get Free of Negative Emotions?

We all need to know how to not just have a good day now and then, but how to find *total* emotional healing and restoration. We must understand how to fill our empty and lonely places with something other than that which will ultimately leave us more empty and lonely than before. We grow weary of battling depression, anxiety, fear, anger, feelings of rejection and failure, and thoughts that we haven't done enough or we've done the wrong thing. We are exhausted by unrelenting self-criticism, shame, confusion, and a chronic lack of fulfillment. God says of these things, "Instead of your shame you shall have double honor, and instead of confusion they shall rejoice in their portion. Therefore in their land they shall possess double; everlasting joy shall be theirs" (Isaiah 61:7). This double honor illustrates the way God is. He not only restores but also gives us far beyond what we hope.

My mother often referred to me with profanity I cannot repeat. I realized many years later that was part of her mental illness. Being locked in a closet contributed to the countless negative emotions I dealt with every day. I don't remember being locked up as a specific punishment for something I'd done; it was more that she didn't want me around. She used to say, "Stay in there until I can stand to see your face."

In later years, when there was no longer a physical closet, I lived in an emotional closet—locked up by the pain and fear in my heart and soul. When I was in my twenties, I tried anything I thought would help me get free of these negative emotions that paralyzed me—alcohol, drugs, occult practices, Eastern religions, and bad relationships. It was all in an attempt to find a way out of my pain and see a reason to live. When I received Jesus, that ended my search for an eternal future and a sense of purpose, but it was just the beginning of finding wholeness.

Gradually, my understanding of who God made me to be, and what I was called to do, became clearer. I developed a sense of peace about where I was in my life, and I had hope about my future—two realizations that had previously eluded me. The three most important steps I took in order to get free of negative emotions were to put God first, fortify myself with God's Word, and pray about everything. You can do this too.

1. *Put God first in every way.* Make a decision to put God first in every area of your life. That means even putting Him before your feelings. Say, "Lord, I will serve You and not my emotions."

2. *Fortify yourself with the Word of God.* You need all the nourishment, rejuvenation, and healing God's Word can give you. "The law of the LORD is perfect, reviving the soul" (Psalm 19:7 NIV). Determine to line your thoughts and emotions up with God's Word. Say, "Lord, what You say in Your Word has a greater influence in my heart than my own feelings."

3. *Pray about everything.* Don't entertain negative emotions as if they are old friends who have arrived as house guests. They don't have

a right to be part of your life anymore. Tell God about each one and ask Him to set you free. The Bible says, "Be anxious for nothing, *but in everything by prayer and supplication, with thanksgiving,* let your requests be made known to God; and the peace of God, which surpasses all understanding, will guard your hearts and minds through Christ Jesus" (Philippians 4:6-7, emphasis added). Say, "Lord, I refuse to give place to negative emotions, so I pray You will take them away. Thank You for protecting my heart and mind, and giving me peace in the process."

If you have struggled with negative emotions, know that God has freedom, healing, and restoration for you. This is a new day and a new beginning, and He is a God of redemption. My journey from bondage to freedom, brokenness to wholeness, and failure to true success didn't happen overnight. It happened step by step. It took 14 years from the time I received the Lord until I was free of emotional pain. I am still on the path of becoming more and more whole because it is a lifelong process. Wrong habits of feeling, acting, or thinking take time to change.

I pray this process happens more quickly for you. But if it doesn't, keep walking toward the wholeness God has for you. Keep saying, "The Lord restores my soul and leads me on the right path" (Psalm 23:3). Walking on any other path in any other direction is a waste of your time and your life.

⤞ PRAYER POWER ⤝

Lord, today I refuse all depression, anxiety, fear, dread, anger, and sadness, for I know they are not from You. By the power of Your Holy Spirit I resist the temptation to see the bad in life, and I ask You to open my eyes to the good. Enable me to sense Your presence at all times, no matter what is happening. My life is in Your hands, and Your love sustains me. May Your joy rise in my heart so fully that it crowds out all that is not of You.

I pray You would evaporate any heaviness in me. Enable me to breathe the fresh air of Your Spirit blowing the dark clouds away. I look to You and not to my problems or the things that aren't perfect in my life. Help me to see anything I dread as a challenge I can rise above, because You enable me.

Thank You that I don't have to live in darkness because You are my light (John 12:46). You have brought me out of darkness and the shadow of death, and broke my chains of bondage (Psalm 107:14). You have delivered me from darkness and brought me into Your kingdom and Your love (Colossians 1:13). Because You are my salvation, I don't have to be afraid (Psalm 27:1). I can call to You and You will save me (Psalm 107:13).

Help me to worship You often. Set me free from all negative emotions that have become a habit. Give me a garment of praise to take away the spirit of heaviness. In Your presence I find fullness of joy (Psalm 16:11).

In Jesus' name I pray.

⤙ WORD POWER ⤚

The LORD redeems the soul of His servants, and none
of those who trust in Him shall be condemned.

PSALM 34:22

"I will restore health to you and heal you
of your wounds," says the LORD.

JEREMIAH 30:17

The Spirit of the Lord GOD is upon Me, because the
LORD has anointed Me to preach good tidings to the
poor; He has sent Me to heal the brokenhearted, to
proclaim liberty to the captives, and the opening of
the prison to those who are bound...to comfort all
who mourn, to console those who mourn in Zion, to

give them beauty for ashes, the oil of joy for mourning,
the garment of praise for the spirit of heaviness;
that they may be called trees of righteousness, the
planting of the LORD, that He may be glorified.

ISAIAH 61:1-3

In the day when I cried out, You answered me,
and made me bold with strength in my soul.

PSALM 138:3

The Lord is my shepherd; I shall not want.
He makes me to lie down in green pastures;
He leads me beside the still waters. He restores my soul;
He leads me in paths of righteousness
for His name's sake.

PSALM 23:1-3

20

TREAT YOUR BODY AS THOUGH IT BELONGS TO GOD

———•◆•———

The way you take care of your body is vital to your true success. However, some people, who are devoted to God in every other part of their life, believe their body is their own private domain and they can do whatever they want with it. But God doesn't see it that way.

God created your body, soul, mind, and spirit. When you receive Jesus, you are filled with the Holy Spirit. He lives in you, enabling you to fulfill your purpose. Your body is His temple, and God expects you to take care of it in honor of Him. "Do you not know that you are the temple of God and that the Spirit of God dwells in you? If anyone defiles the temple of God, God will destroy him. For the temple of God is holy, which temple you are" (1 Corinthians 3:16-17).

Your body is holy because God's Holy Spirit dwells in you. And God will destroy anyone who destroys His temple. This is serious business.

God also says, "My people are destroyed for lack of knowledge" (Hosea 4:6). I believe we are often sick and dying because we are ignorant of proper body care. Our lifestyle choices and habits take us far away from the life of health and rejuvenation God created us to have.

We suffer in our physical body because we do not live God's way. We must learn how to take care of our body in order to enjoy the life of purpose God has for us.

Jesus came as our Healer because He knew we would need healing. We can't always do everything right and our body often breaks down, but that doesn't mean we should abdicate our responsibility to take care of our own body.

If you have never been taught God's way to care for your body, a number of excellent books are available on the subject. Find several of them and learn about a healthy lifestyle that works for you. You must take steps to educate yourself on this. You cannot do nothing and expect to live in good health.

There are many people who know the right way to care for their body but choose not to do it. They treat their body badly and care little about what God wants. This is a destructive path, guaranteed to fail because of flagrant disregard for God's ways. We can't keep poisoning ourselves and expecting God to give us the antidote. It doesn't work that way.

What You Can Do to Take Care of God's Temple

Here are some simple yet practical things you can do to be a good steward over the body God gave you.

Think of Your Body as the Foundation of Your Life and Ministry

Present your body to the Lord as a living sacrifice and ask Him to help you care for it in a way that is pleasing to Him. Sickness takes away from your life and the purposes God has for you. If you treat it right, your body was created to be self-repairing. You cannot serve the Lord on earth without it.

Ask God to Show You Where You Need to Have Balance

The Bible says, "The man who fears the Lord will avoid all [extremes]" (Ecclesiastes 7:18 NIV). Do you work too hard and don't get enough rest? Do you put food in your body that you know is bad for you? Do you not get enough fresh air and sunshine for eleven months and three weeks of the year, and then bake in the sun for a week until you are overcooked? Do you drink a lot of chemical-filled, sugary soft drinks and very little water? Do you live life in the fast lane and don't take time to pray every day? Do you have time for the television but not for the Bible? Do you refuse to exercise because you think you are one of the few who can get away with it? Do you allow yourself to be overweight without considering the consequences? Do you seldom fast and pray in order to break these bad habits?

If you said yes to any of these questions above, ask God to break down the strongholds of bad body care habits you are struggling with. He will do that. You don't have to face this seemingly overwhelming task alone. God will help you, guide you, and sustain you in the process.

Ask God to Show You if Stress Is Affecting You Negatively

Pray that God will help you to eliminate or handle the stress in your life. Ask Him to enable you to "be content whatever the circumstances" (Philippians 4:11 NIV). Remember that only God is perfect and can make things perfect. We can only do what we can do, and then we have to let it go at that. Don't let stress bring you to the point of depletion and exhaustion.

Eat Right and Fortify Your Body

You can do a lot to keep yourself healthy by watching what you eat. If you eat badly, your body will break down. God has given us guidelines and foods for good health, and He expects us to be responsible with our eating. Chronic pain and debilitating sickness are not God's will for your life. Ask Him to show you what you can do to make changes in your eating habits that will promote healing. Present your body to the Lord and ask Him to lead you to the right people to help you (Romans 12:1).

Find the Rest God Has for You

If you are not resting, you are not obeying God. In fact, one of the reasons we don't sleep well at night is because we are not living His way during the day. He gives us rest when we live His way. Deep, restful sleep is extremely important if you want to have good health. When you are at peace in your life, and you eat good health-filled foods, get proper exercise, drink plenty of pure water, and fast and pray periodically, you will find that sleep comes naturally.

If you are the other extreme and have to sleep all the time, then something is out of balance in your body. God gives us a time to sleep and a time to be awake and active. A body that is healthy does not become confused about this. Also, if you work too hard and can't sleep at night, then some changes need to be made. The Bible says, "It is vain for you to rise up early, to sit up late, to eat the bread of sorrows; for so He gives His beloved sleep" (Psalm 127:2). When you are asleep, your body cleanses itself and rebuilds and repairs. Don't shortchange the time it needs to do that well.

Get Regular Exercise

We don't feel well when there are toxins in the body. One of the greatest advantages of exercise is that it frees the body of toxins. A lack of exercise can be the cause of lack of sleep at night. A lack of sleep doesn't give the body time to cleanse and repair itself. We have to use the body God gave us in order to stay healthy. When it doesn't have enough activity, the cleansing and building process cannot happen fully. When it comes to exercise, don't do nothing.

Observe the Sabbath Day of Rest God Commanded Us to Take

If God took a day of rest for Himself, and He said that *we* should as well, I think we should trust Him on that (Exodus 20:8-10). Take that day once a week and don't work, don't worry about your bills, or think about what needs cleaning or fixing, or be consumed with all the obligations you have to fulfill. Spend that day with the Lord so He can refresh you. Spend time at church or with your family, take a nap, or eat a meal with friends. Take a break from your daily schedule and spend time doing what you enjoy. Whatever you do, include God in it. The Sabbath day is a reward for your body, mind, soul, and spirit.

Thank God for the Gift of Your Body

Don't criticize your body for what it won't do, can't do, or doesn't want to do, but instead thank God for what it *can* do. Thank God that you can see, hear, talk, move, walk, or whatever it is you are able to do.

Give up the attitude that says, "This is my body and I'll do what I want with it." The truth is, you were bought by the suffering and blood of Jesus. You are a clay pot that God has filled with His Spirit and uses for His glory. "We have this treasure in earthen vessels, that the excellence of the power may be of God and not of us" (2 Corinthians 4:7). Be grateful your body can be used for the glory of God and cooperate in keeping it well.

What God Can Do to Help You Care for Your Body

Here are some things God can do to help you be a good steward over the body He gave you.

God Can Answer Prayer

Jesus said that whatever we ask in His name He will do for us (John 14:13). Don't try to care for your body without His help. Pray about every aspect of it. Ask Him to show you what to do and enable you to do it. Ask God to help you stay well.

God Can Do Miracles

Jesus is your Healer. And He will do miracles of healing in response to your prayers. But that doesn't give you permission to not care for your body. (More about this in chapter 21, "Trust in Your Healer.")

God Can Give You a Heart of Peace

Your peace comes from God, and you should seek Him for it. Peace is healing and rejuvenating, and it will greatly affect your health. "A heart at peace gives life to the body" (Proverbs 14:30 NIV). Ask God to help you learn to live in His peace.

God Can Bless You When You Walk His Way

As you take steps of obedience with regard to body care, God will bless the steps you take. "Blessed are all who fear the LORD, who walk in his ways. You will eat the fruit of your labor; blessings and prosperity will be yours" (Psalm 128:1-2 NIV). A big part of prosperity is enjoying good health.

When you ask God to help you properly care for your body, He will open your eyes to anything you might have been doing wrong. "The LORD gives sight to the blind" (Psalm 146:8 NIV). He will show you the steps to take. Serve Him by doing what He says.

Always remember that your body is the Lord's. Have respect for it out of respect for Him. Love your body because you love Him who created you.

✦ PRAYER POWER ✦

Lord, I commit my body to You as the temple of Your Holy Spirit. Teach me how to care for it properly. Show me how I should eat and what I should avoid. Take away all desire for food that is harmful to me. Give me balance and wisdom. Help me to purify myself from everything that contaminates my body and spirit out of reverence for You (2 Corinthians 7:1).

Enable me to live Your way so that I can dwell in the peace You have for me. Show me where I allow unnecessary stress to rule in my life, and help me to take steps to alleviate it. Teach me to simplify my life so that I can live better and healthier. Enable me to rest at night, as You created me to do. Make my heart to be at peace so that my body is rejuvenated" (Proverbs 14:30 NIV).

I pray You would enable me to "make no provision for the

flesh, to fulfill its lusts" (Romans 13:14). Help me to exercise as I should so that my body stays cleansed, active, and strong. Where I have long-entrenched bad habits when it comes to proper care for my body, I ask You to reveal them all to me and enable me to take the necessary steps to get free.

Help me to love and appreciate my body and not be critical of it. Enable me to choose life (Deuteronomy 30:19). Even though my flesh and heart may fail, You are the strength of my heart forever (Psalm 73:26). Enable me to go from "strength to strength" (Psalm 84:7).

In Jesus' name I pray.

⇢ Word Power ⇠

Therefore, I urge you, brothers, in view of God's mercy, to offer your bodies as living sacrifices, holy and pleasing to God—this is your spiritual act of worship.

Romans 12:1 niv

I will praise You, for I am fearfully and wonderfully made.

Psalm 139:14

Whether you eat or drink or whatever you do, do it all for the glory of God.

1 Corinthians 10:31 niv

He will die for lack of discipline, led astray by his own great folly.

Proverbs 5:23 niv

There is a way that seems right to a man, but in the end it leads to death.

Proverbs 16:25 niv

→ 21 ←

TRUST IN YOUR HEALER

————◆◆◆————

God is the God of miracles. He can do miracles in response to our prayers. Thank God for doctors, but even *they* know that medicine can't do everything. There are many times when we need a miracle of healing. And that's why Jesus came as our Healer.

If you have been told in the past that God doesn't do miracles today, realize that it doesn't say that in the Scriptures. God says, "For I am the Lord, I do not change" (Malachi 3:6). The writer of the book of Hebrews said, "Jesus Christ is the same yesterday, today, and forever" (Hebrews 13:8). Jesus *is*—not Jesus *was*.

If miracles have ceased, then why did James tell the church to pray for the sick? "Is anyone among you sick? Let him call for the elders of the church, and let them pray over him, anointing him with oil in the name of the Lord. And the prayer of faith will save the sick, and the Lord will raise him up. And if he has committed sins, he will be forgiven" (James 5:14-15).

Jesus said, "Most assuredly, I say to you, *he who believes in Me,* the works that I do he will do also; and greater works than these he will do, because I go to My Father" (John 14:12, emphasis added). Jesus did *not* say, "Just you disciples who believe in Me."

Jesus also said, "Assuredly, I say to you, if you have faith as a mustard seed, you will say to this mountain, 'Move from here to there,' and it will move; and nothing will be impossible for you" (Matthew 17:20). Is there any greater mountain than sickness that doesn't heal?

God gives each of us a certain amount of faith to start with, but our faith *increases* as we read God's Word and act on it (Romans 12:3). Our faith can grow big enough to move a mountain. Jesus said, "These signs will follow those who believe: In My name they will cast out demons… they will lay hands on the sick, and they will recover" (Mark 16:17-18). There were no cutoff dates or expiration dates on these Scriptures. Nowhere does it say, "Once the apostles are dead, forget about seeing anymore miracles. They are not going to happen."

Your faith in God invites and releases God's power to work in your life. Don't put faith in your ability to have faith; put your faith in God's ability to heal. If your faith feels weak to you, ask God to increase it. Believe that there is nothing too hard for God (Mark 10:27). If you want to see a miracle, lay hold of this Scripture until it becomes part of your mind and heart.

Preparing Your Heart for a Miracle of Healing

Here are some things you can do to make your heart ready for healing.

Prepare Your Heart by Reading God's Word and Increasing Your Faith

It is possible to find healing as you simply read the Word of God. "He sent His word and healed them, and delivered them from their destructions" (Psalm 107:20). Our destructions could be our willful disobedience to God's ways and will. Too often people don't pray until something terrible happens and they want God to fix it. I believe that sometimes severe sickness can bring us back from our own spiritual decline or apathy and jar us out of disobedience.

God's Word has more power than any disease or injury you are facing. "My son, give attention to my words; incline your ear to my sayings. Do not let them depart from your eyes; keep them in the midst of your heart; for they are life to those who find them, and *health to all their flesh*" (Proverbs 4:20-22, emphasis added).

Memorize Scriptures about healing, for they will be life to you. "Unless Your law had been my delight, I would then have perished in my affliction. I will never forget Your precepts, for by them You have given me life" (Psalm 119:92-93).

Prepare Your Heart with Prayer

When we cry out to the Lord for healing, He hears us. Sometimes He heals right away. Sometimes our healing happens over the course of a long convalescence. Sometimes it doesn't happen the way we prayed. That is not to say when someone does not get healed in response to prayer it proves that God does not heal today. Jesus did *not* say, "With God all things are possible only for this month, or just as long as the apostles are alive. After that, you're on your own."

Prepare Your Heart by Obeying the Commands of God

Separate yourself from all that is opposed to God and His ways. "My son, do not forget my law, but let your heart keep my commands; *for length of days and long life and peace they will add to you*" (Proverbs 3:1-2, emphasis added). Choose to be humble and give reverence to God. "Do not be wise in your own eyes; fear the LORD and depart from evil. *It will be health to your flesh and strength to your bones*" (Proverbs 3:7-8, emphasis added).

Prepare Your Heart with Fasting

God said that when we fast many things will happen, one of which is healing. "Then your light shall break forth like the morning, your healing shall spring forth speedily, and your righteousness shall go before you; the glory of the LORD shall be your rear guard" (Isaiah 58:8). That is one of many important things that happens when we fast, and perhaps the lack of fasting is why many people get sick. (More about that in chapter 27, "Fast and Pray to Win.")

What Jesus Said About Healing

A blind man begging by the road cried out to Jesus when He walked by, saying, "Jesus, Son of David, have mercy on me!" Jesus knew that the man was blind and that he wanted more than anything else to be able to see. But still Jesus asked, "What do you want Me to do for you?" The blind man said, "Lord, that I may receive my sight." Then Jesus said, "Receive your sight; your faith has made you well" (Luke 18:38-42). God knows what we need and what we want, but He wants us to ask. That's why it is good to pray specifically. Ask God specifically for what you want in the way of healing. Then have faith in His ability and desire to heal. Proclaim His Word about healing until you see the situation resolved, no matter how long it takes.

I know God does miracles because I have seen so many of them in my own life. I have been close to death a number of times, and miraculously I have survived. I know in each incident it was the hand of God in response to prayer. You have to believe with all your heart that nothing is impossible with God. "Jesus looked at them and said, 'With men it is impossible, but not with God; *for with God all things are possible'* " (Mark 10:27, emphasis added).

Healing is not something we *demand* from God. God does not heal everyone. Why He heals one and not another is entirely His call (John 5:1-10). He is sovereign and does what He wills. We can't set up a formula and demand that God will do what we want. Prayer isn't telling God what to do, remember? Prayer is communicating the desires of your heart to God and then putting them in His hands to do what He wills. But just because God does not heal *everyone* doesn't mean that He does not heal *anyone.* He does heal. When He does not heal, He has a purpose for it. And we have to trust Him in that.

Jesus paid for our healing on the cross (Isaiah 53:4-5). He took our infirmities upon Himself and bore our sicknesses (Matthew 8:16-17). Why would He purchase our healing with His own suffering on the cross if He didn't want to heal us? "He himself bore our sins in his body on the tree, so that we might die to sins and live for righteousness; *by his wounds you have been healed"* (1 Peter 2:24 NIV, emphasis added). Why did He go to all that trouble? Why is He referred to as our Healer if He didn't intend to heal anyone?

People came to Jesus for healing, and they begged Him to let them touch the edge of His garment. "All who touched Him were healed" (Mark 6:56 NIV). We, too, need to touch Jesus to receive healing. In order to touch Him, we must be *in touch* with Him.

Many times Jesus referred to someone's faith being instrumental in their healing. For example, the centurion who asked Jesus to heal his servant also told Jesus that it wasn't necessary for Him to go *to* his servant. He said, "Just say the word, and my servant will be healed" (Matthew 8:8 NIV). Jesus was astonished by his faith and responded, "'It will be done just as you believed it would.' And his servant was healed in that very hour" (verse 13 NIV).

There Is Power in the Name of Jesus to Heal

When Peter said to a lame man, "In the name of Jesus Christ of Nazareth, rise up and walk," the man leaped up and walked for the first time (Acts 3:6-8). Peter explained to the people watching in amazement what had happened, saying, "His name, through faith in His name, has made this man strong, whom you see and know. Yes, the faith which comes through Him has given him this perfect soundness in the presence of you all" (Acts 3:16). What Peter was saying was that it wasn't by any power of his own that this man was healed. It was the power of Jesus' name that brought healing. And it is prayer that directs that power.

When you put your faith in Jesus and the power of His name to heal, healing can happen. Confess that Jesus is Lord and that He has given you power and authority in His name to command infirmity and sickness to go. Don't let anyone weaken your faith in Jesus and His ability to heal by telling you that He only healed people back when He was on earth but not now.

Jesus was the Healer then, He is the Healer now, and He will always be our Healer.

⤙ Prayer Power ⤚

Lord, I thank You for Your healing power on my behalf. Thank You for sending forth Your Word to heal me (Psalm 107:20). I believe You, Jesus, are the living Word. You paid the price on the cross to purchase healing for me. You took my infirmities and bore my sickness. There is healing in Your name, and I believe You are my healer.

Thank You for Your written Word which comes alive in my heart as I read it, speak it, or hear it. I pray Your Word in my heart will be medicine for my body. I praise You, Lord, for all Your promises of safety, protection, and healing. I choose to believe Your Word and have faith in You and Your power to heal.

I pray for health and healing upon my body. Restore health to me and heal me of all my wounds (Jeremiah 30:17). Enlarge my faith in You and Your name so that I can lay hold of the healing You paid for on the cross. Help me not to give up praying until I see the healing You have for me. I know that when You heal me, I am truly healed (Jeremiah 17:14).

Teach me how to pray in power and faith for the healing of others. Lead me and teach me to obey You in this way. Every time I pray for someone else, hear my prayer and answer by touching that person with Your healing power. Show me how to pray so that You can do a miracle, not only in my life but also in the lives of other people.

In Jesus' name I pray.

⤙ Word Power ⤚

Surely He has borne our griefs and carried our
sorrows; yet we esteemed Him stricken, smitten
by God, and afflicted. But He was wounded
for our transgressions, He was bruised for our

iniquities; the chastisement for our peace was
upon Him, and by His stripes we are healed.

Isaiah 53:4-5

To you who fear My name the Sun of Righteousness
shall arise with healing in His wings.

Malachi 4:2

Bless the Lord, O my soul; and all that is within
me, bless His holy name! Bless the Lord, O my
soul, and forget not all His benefits: who forgives
all your iniquities, who heals all your diseases.

Psalm 103:1-3

Heal me, O Lord, and I shall be healed; save
me, and I shall be saved, for You are my praise.

Jeremiah 17:14

If you diligently heed the voice of the Lord your
God and do what is right in His sight, give ear to His
commandments and keep all His statutes, I will put
none of the diseases on you which I have brought on
the Egyptians. For I am the Lord who heals you.

Exodus 15:26

→ 22 ←

SAY "NO WAY"
TO TEMPTATION

Part of the Lord's Prayer says, "Do not lead us into temptation, but deliver us from the evil one" (Matthew 6:13).

When I was a new believer, I used to wonder about that. Would God actually lead us into temptation, so we would need to pray that He won't? But as I read more about this in the Bible, I saw that God cannot be tempted, nor will He tempt us. "Let no one say when he is tempted, 'I am tempted by God'; for God cannot be tempted by evil, nor does He Himself tempt anyone" (James 1:13).

What we are really praying in the Lord's Prayer is, "God, lead us *away* from temptation." It would also be like saying, "Lord, when I am tempted to get off the path, I need Your help to stay headed in the right direction. Help me to walk away from anything that tempts me away from You." We are asking God to give us strength to stand strong against the evil one or anything within us that would entice us off the moral ground God has for us to stand on.

Temptation means an enticement to do evil. God does not *entice* us to do wrong. The enemy will tempt us from the outside; our flesh will tempt us from within. God does, however, allow us to be *tested* by temptation.

Our flesh is our lowest nature, where our sinful desires find a place to lodge. It is our weakest part. And even though in our spirit we want to do what's right, we can still be overcome by our weak nature and allow temptation to overpower us. Jesus said, "Watch and pray, lest you enter into temptation. The spirit indeed is willing, but the flesh is weak" (Matthew 26:41). We can be enticed in our flesh to do wrong. But the key Jesus gives us to avoid that is to be watchful and prayerful.

We have to be aware that we can be lured away from God's best, so we have to watch for signs of that happening and continually pray that God will help us resist it.

When we stand strong, resist temptation, and endure the time of tempting, we receive a reward from God. "Blessed is the man who endures temptation; for when he has been approved, he will receive the crown of life which the Lord has promised to those who love Him" (James 1:12). This promise of blessings is realized not only in the life to come, but in this life as well.

Every time I have come to the brink of major breakthrough in my life as a believer, I have been attacked by the enemy with temptation to believe one of his lies or to violate one of God's laws. I know that the enemy has come to destroy what God wants to do through me. What I have done every time is to lay all else aside and go before the Lord and pray. I ask Him to take the temptation out of my life and release me from the hold of it. I ask Him to reveal anything in my flesh that would allow for such a struggle. I choose to believe that the power of the Holy Spirit in me is far greater than whatever I am facing.

If you experience temptation to do, say, or think anything that you know is not of the Lord, recognize that you will not endure beyond what others have experienced. That's because God will not allow you to be tempted beyond what you are able to handle (1 Corinthians 10:13).

How to Resist Temptation

Here are some things that will help you stand strong against temptation.

Prayer Will Help You Persevere

Luke says that Jesus "spoke a parable to them, that men always ought to pray and not lose heart" (Luke 18:1). We cannot allow ourselves to become weak and entertain thoughts we know are not right. We must pray about even the slightest hint of temptation.

Be extremely cautious when you are trying to help someone else resist temptation. You can get caught in the same sin as the person you are trying to help. This is part of the secret war the enemy wages upon us in the area of our mind. You think you can keep your thoughts from turning into action, but the truth is, you cannot *think* of evil and not get hooked by it. The mere thought of it, if given more than a moment, can lodge in your mind. Paul says, "If a man is overtaken in any trespass, you who are spiritual restore such a one in a spirit of gentleness, considering yourself lest you also be tempted" (Galatians 6:1). "If sinners entice you, do not consent" (Proverbs 1:10). This is biblical support for any "Just Say No" campaign. No matter what the situation, pray fervently.

The Word of God Will Strengthen You

God's Word is a guide—a light on the right path. It exposes anything that is wrong. It emboldens you to resist temptation. It encourages you to stand strong. It increases your faith to believe that God has secured your victory in this battle. In order to resist any temptation that comes from the enemy, you have to use your most powerful weapon, which is God's Word. That's what Jesus did, and if it's good enough for Him, it is certainly good enough for you and me.

Jesus had been fasting for 40 days and 40 nights when Satan came to Him and said, "If You are the Son of God, command that these stones become bread" (Matthew 4:3). Satan thought he could tempt Jesus to eat before it was time, but Jesus answered him with the Word of God. He said, "It is written, 'Man shall not live by bread alone, but by every word that proceeds from the mouth of God'" (Matthew 4:4).

The devil tried again to tempt Jesus by taking Him up to the pinnacle of the temple and telling Him to prove He was the Son of God by throwing Himself down to the ground. Satan even used the Word of God *against* Jesus by quoting, "He shall give His angels charge over you" and "in their hands they shall bear you up" (Matthew 4:6). In other words, "Go ahead and jump, Jesus, and if You really are the Son of God, angels will catch You." Jesus resisted him with the Word of God, saying, "It is written again, 'You shall not tempt the Lord your God'" (Matthew 4:7).

Satan tried a third time by offering Jesus the world if He would just bow down and worship him. But Jesus again quoted the Word of God, saying, "Away with you, Satan! For it is written, 'You shall worship the LORD your God, and Him only you shall serve'" (Matthew 4:10). And that's when Satan finally left, and "angels came and ministered to Him" (Matthew 4:11).

Jesus was tempted by the devil to do what He knew was not right. He resisted the devil by quoting the Word of God. We can do the same and it will be just as powerful. When you are tempted by the enemy to sin in order to prove something or gain the world, quote the Word of God.

Jesus empathizes with you when you are tempted. So call on His name and speak the Word of God in the face of the temptation, and He will enable you to overcome. "We do not have a High Priest who cannot sympathize with our weaknesses, but was in all points tempted as we are, yet without sin" (Hebrews 4:15). Because Jesus "has suffered, being tempted, He is able to aid those who are tempted" (Hebrews 2:18).

The enemy will always try to get you off the path God has for you. This is especially true when you are about to have breakthrough—when you are moving into a new thing God is doing in your life or your ministry is about to open up to a new level of effectiveness. In fact, you can expect the enemy to tempt you in the area where you are most vulnerable. Be prepared for that. Find the verses of Scripture that best meet your need to withstand temptation.

EXAMPLES OF BATTLE-READY SCRIPTURE

When I am tempted to immorality. "This is the will of God, your sanctification: that you should abstain from sexual immorality; that each of you should know how to possess his own vessel in sanctification and honor, not in passion of lust, like the Gentiles who do not know God" (1 Thessalonians 4:3-5).

When I am tempted to lie. "A false witness will not go unpunished, and he who speaks lies will not escape" (Proverbs 19:5).

When I am tempted to disobey God. "Do not enter the path of the wicked, and do not walk in the way of evil" (Proverbs 4:14).

When I am tempted to give in to lustful thoughts. "The righteousness of the upright will deliver them, but the unfaithful will be caught by their lust" (Proverbs 11:6).

When I am tempted to think no one will know. "There is no creature hidden from His sight, but all things are naked and open to the eyes of Him to whom we must give account" (Hebrews 4:13).

When I am tempted to go with my feelings. "He who trusts in his own heart is a fool, but whoever walks wisely will be delivered" (Proverbs 28:26).

Temptations, such as lust or greed, are a strong force. We cannot handle them on our own. Refuse to let the enemy destroy your life. "Abstain from fleshly lusts which war against the soul" (1 Peter 2:11). Don't let yourself desire something you know is wrong. Bring it to God. "Let us therefore come boldly to the throne of grace, that we may obtain mercy and find grace to help in time of need" (Hebrews 4:16).

Jesus prayed for His disciples that God would "keep them from the evil one" (John 17:15). How much more should we pray this for ourselves and for those we care about?

❖ Prayer Power ❖

Lord, I pray You would lead me far away from all temptation to do or think anything that is not pleasing to You. Help me to always know what is right and enable me to do it. Deliver me from all attacks of the evil one, who tries to entice me away from what is good in Your sight. I pray that the weakness of my flesh will be overcome by the strength and power of Your Spirit.

I choose to be God controlled and not flesh controlled. I know I am dead to sin but alive in Christ Jesus, and therefore I will not allow sin to reign in me. I refuse to give in to the lust of my flesh for anything other than what is Your will for me to have. I declare that sin will not have dominion over me, for by Your power and grace I can resist it (Romans 6:11-14). I know I can stand strong if I stand on the truth of Your Word. Help me to know Your Word well and remember it at all times.

Lord, I thank You that You will not allow me to be tempted beyond what I am able to handle. Thank You for making a way for me to escape temptation (1 Corinthians 10:13). I turn to You, Lord, and ask that by the power of Your Holy Spirit You will help me to withstand any onslaught of the enemy. Teach me to take "the shield of faith" with which I will be able to "quench all the fiery darts of the wicked one" (Ephesians 6:16).

In Jesus' name I pray.

❖ Word Power ❖

No temptation has overtaken you except such as is common to man; but God is faithful, who will not allow you to be tempted beyond what you are able, but with the temptation will also make the way of escape, that you may be able to bear it.

1 Corinthians 10:13

Each one is tempted when he is drawn away
by his own desires and enticed. Then, when
desire has conceived, it gives birth to sin; and
sin, when it is full-grown, brings forth death.

JAMES 1:14-15

Those who desire to be rich fall into temptation and a
snare, and into many foolish and harmful lusts which
drown men in destruction and perdition. For the
love of money is a root of all kinds of evil, for which
some have strayed from the faith in their greediness,
and pierced themselves through with many sorrows.

1 TIMOTHY 6:9-10

Be sober, be vigilant; because your adversary the
devil walks about like a roaring lion, seeking
whom he may devour. Resist him, steadfast in
the faith, knowing that the same sufferings are
experienced by your brotherhood in the world.

1 PETER 5:8-9

Reckon yourselves to be dead indeed to sin, but
alive to God in Christ Jesus our Lord. Therefore
do not let sin reign in your mortal body, that you
should obey it in its lusts. And do not present your
members as instruments of unrighteousness to
sin, but present yourselves to God as being alive
from the dead, and your members as instruments of
righteousness to God. For sin shall not have dominion
over you, for you are not under law but under grace.

ROMANS 6:11-14

✣ 23 ✣

STEP OUT OF
DESTRUCTIVE
RELATIONSHIPS

———◆◦┼◦◆———

Good relationships are crucial to our success in life. We can't live well without them. Studies have been done on the importance of positive social support systems with regard to our health. The conclusions have been that good relationships contribute to better health and a lower death rate. That is one good reason why we should pray for each one of our relationships to be uplifting, edifying, encouraging, and always glorifying to God.

The Bible says that two people in a friendship or good relationship should speak the truth in *love* and not beat the other up with negative personal opinions (Ephesians 4:15). A good friend should not be always changeable, so you never know how they are going to react or what they are going to do next (Proverbs 24:21-22). A good friend is not always angry about something (Proverbs 22:24-25). I have found that too many people—women especially—will put up with relationships in which the other person is changeable, angry, negative, and generally destructive to their well-being.

We know when we are in a good relationship. And we know when we have a relationship that is troubling. But we don't often know how much damage is being done to us when we continue in a destructive relationship. I have known women who I believe have died of an illness *because* they did not step out of their destructive relationship with their husband. I am not saying they should have gotten divorced, necessarily. I am saying they should never have let things go on so long without addressing the issues that were destructive for them. I may sound as though I am blaming the victim, but I am not at all. I just know how some of us will put up with negativity in a relationship because we think we deserve it or we are trying to be a martyr or we are afraid to confront the other person. And that is not what God wants for us at all.

God is forgiving, and we are supposed to forgive others as He forgives us. But He doesn't say we have to keep subjecting ourselves to abuse, hurt, pain, fear, or mistreatment. He said to turn the other cheek, but He didn't say to permit others to make us sick, anxious, depressed, or traumatized. We can refuse to allow sin, and the destruction that comes with it, to go on.

While good relationships enhance our lives, bad ones are far more damaging than we think. We must do what we can to protect and nurture the good ones but stop tolerating the bad ones. Those relationships are the ones that constantly make you upset and miserable.

I'm not saying you have to get rid of every relationship that goes through a difficult time. What I *am* saying is that when a relationship becomes destructive to you, put a stop to it. Don't permit it to carry on like that. It is not of God, and it doesn't glorify Him.

Stepping Out of a Destructive Relationship

If you have a relationship with a friend, family member, neighbor, coworker, or employer that is detrimental to you, you need to separate yourself from that person in order to be free of it. While you cannot control how everyone will treat you, you *can* control how they *continue* to treat you.

You can't make a person be any other way than the way they are determined to be, but you *can* step out of a destructive relationship and refuse to allow someone to go on mistreating you and taking away your joy. If someone continually causes you to feel bad about yourself, your family, or your life, release that person to God and pray for him or her from afar.

This is not a license to run from every problem and refuse to work things out. This is letting go of a bad situation you believe *cannot* be worked out. Stepping out of a destructive relationship doesn't mean you have to desert that person completely. It means you refuse to allow them to be destructive to *you*. You no longer allow that person to bring negativity into your life.

Don't think for a moment that you deserve to be treated badly in a relationship. You don't! Do not let yourself be so emotionally needy that you allow abuse of any kind. People who would not tolerate physical abuse sometimes fail to see when verbal or emotional abuse is happening. They know they feel bad when they are around the other person, and they see how his or her words wound their soul, but they don't realize that by permitting it they are allowing themselves to be destroyed.

Those of us who had extremely negative relationships growing up— as I did with my mother—have a hard time understanding what a normal relationship is. We are able to see it in others, but we don't know how to get it ourselves. If we are in a destructive relationship and we are emotionally broken, it is harder for us to get free of it. We tend to think that it's the only kind of relationship we deserve, but that's not true. The truth is, the only way we can grow and develop is in a loving environment, a place where we feel safe.

In all destructive relationships, it's not just someone having a bad attitude on a bad day; it's someone constantly making you feel bad. If you have a person like that in your life, ask God to show you what to do about it. If possible, tell that person clearly how you feel—not in a confrontational manner, but in a "come, let us reason together" kind of way. If that person is too hardheaded to listen or too hard-hearted to want to change, don't stay in it. Combating someone else's strong will is not your job. Even God won't do it, and He is far better equipped than you are.

Just remember, if you are not married to that person, then the good news is that *you are not married to that person.* You don't have to stay in the relationship and act as though you are.

When the Most Difficult Relationship Is with Your Spouse

Of course, when your most difficult relationship is with your spouse, that is different. You have made a covenant with your spouse—you have spoken vows of devotion, commitment, and love before God—and you owe it to each other and God to do all you can to make things right. You have to do whatever is necessary to save, renew, restore, or resurrect your marriage because that is the will of God. You must pray that God will pour out His Spirit on both of you and open your hearts to His love, wisdom, and purpose in your lives together.

The Bible says we are to "therefore receive one another, just as Christ also received us, to the glory of God" (Romans 15:7). If a married couple can truly receive one another as Christ receives them—with forgiveness and love—then the power of God can transform their marriage and their lives. But if one person insists on being abusive to the other, that changes things. If you continue to live with an abusive person, you're always thinking, *If I do this, will it upset him (her)? Is there anything I can say that will not make him (her) mad? What is he (she) going to be like today?*

If you are in an abusive marriage, don't sacrifice who God made you to be and what you know is right in the Lord by tolerating it. If you do, that will destroy both of you. Allowing a spouse to abuse you makes you an accomplice to his or her sin. Pray and pray about it until you know what to do. If you feel you are in danger, remove yourself from the relationship until something changes. God did not call you to be grieved, threatened, beaten down, damaged, or destroyed. Get away from the abuser until your spouse wakes up, repents, and starts drastically changing his or her ways. If you are in doubt about what to do, seek help from God and good Christian counselors.

Don't enable your spouse to sin by allowing him or her to continually abuse you. Don't allow him or her to bring out the worst in you. God has better for both of you than that.

In a good relationship, you should build one another up and give each other a sense of support and well-being. And no relationship should require so much of you that you have nothing left for anyone else and no time to do what God is calling you to do. If a relationship is grieving you, ask God to show you what to do about it. I know He won't say to do nothing.

Ask God to be in charge of *all* your relationships. Pray that the enemy cannot come in and break up the good ones, and that you will recognize the ones sucking the life out of you and stealing your peace. It's one thing if you have a relationship that can be repaired, but if you feel as though you are beating your head against a brick wall, ask God about moving on. Some relationships are worth trying to make right, but some will never be any different than they are and may only get worse. You have to decide if it's worth the time and effort it will take and who you will be neglecting in the process.

⤖ Prayer Power ⬸

Lord, I thank You for the people You have put into my life. Make all my good relationships stronger. Help me to handle the difficult ones in a way that pleases You. Remove any hopelessly destructive relationship from my life by either changing it for the better or by taking that person out of my life.

Give me wisdom about the friends I choose. Help me not to ever be in a relationship with anyone who will lead me off the path You have for me. Give me discernment to recognize when a person is not a good influence.

If there is any relationship I have that is destructive for either of us, enable us both to change in order to make it better or help us to let it go. I pray You would send people into my life who are godly, wise, and strong in their knowledge of You. Help us to contribute to the quality of each other's lives. Teach me to be a good friend to others. Enable me to love others as myself (Galatians 5:14).

Remind me to always be quick to forgive in any relationship.

Give me the ability to let things go and not carry grudges against anyone. Help me to always exhibit Your love to others. Heal any strain between me and anyone else. Show me the relationships that are worth fighting for, and help me to see when a relationship will always be destructive no matter what I do. Enable me to move with the leading of Your Holy Spirit in this. I ask You to be in charge of all of my relationships so that they will be what You want them to be.

In Jesus' name I pray.

✦ WORD POWER ✦

You, brethren, have been called to liberty; only do not use liberty as an opportunity for the flesh, but through love serve one another. For all the law is fulfilled in one word, even in this: "You shall love your neighbor as yourself."

GALATIANS 5:13-14

A friend loves at all times.

PROVERBS 17:17

Make no friendship with an angry man, and with a furious man do not go, lest you learn his ways and set a snare for your soul.

PROVERBS 22:24-25

If a wise man contends with a foolish man, whether the fool rages or laughs, there is no peace.

PROVERBS 29:9

Two are better than one, because they have a good reward for their labor. For if they fall, one will lift up his companion. But woe to him who is alone when he falls, for he has no one to help him up.

ECCLESIASTES 4:9-10

SPEAK WORDS
THAT BRING LIFE

Words matter. The words we speak have a greater impact than we think they do. The way we talk about ourselves and our lives affects us more than we know. And our words spoken to others not only bring life or death to *them,* but also to *us.* "He who guards his mouth preserves his life, but he who opens wide his lips shall have destruction" (Proverbs 13:3).

We will one day have to explain every careless word we have spoken. Jesus said, "I say to you that for every idle word men may speak, they will give account of it in the day of judgment" (Matthew 12:36). Who wants to explain to God why we said some of the stupid things we've said? Better to guard our mouths and ask God to help us to speak words that bring life.

Correcting a Heart Problem

Much is said in the Bible about the way we speak. First of all, our words are indicative of a heart condition. Jesus said that "out of the abundance of the heart the mouth speaks" (Matthew 12:34). Speaking words that heal and bless signify a good heart. But speaking words that are cruel, insensitive, deceptive, dishonest, or careless is a sign of a serious heart problem.

The way to combat this kind of heart problem is to fill your heart with truth—which means the Word of God. When we speak words to or about ourselves that infect our mind with untruth, it affects our life more than we know. If we are speaking lies about ourselves, such as, "I'm never going to get anywhere," "I can't do anything right," or, "There is no way out of my problems," this kind of self-talk has a negative impact on us. Even if we don't really believe those things at first, we can talk ourselves into them. We may think, *It's just words,* but it's more than that. The Bible says, "Death and life are in the power of the tongue, and those who love it will eat its fruit" (Proverbs 18:21). Everything we say promotes either life or death in our own life and in the lives of those to whom we speak.

Ask yourself if the words you speak to others are inspired by God, your own fleshly fears, negative attitudes and thoughts, or the enemy. The Bible says, "You are snared by the words of your mouth" (Proverbs 6:2). Don't let the words you speak set up a trap for you to fall into.

In order to have true success, you must speak the truth of God about yourself and your life. In order to do that, you need a healthy heart that overflows with an abundance of God's love. When your heart is right, the words you speak will be also.

Stop Negative Self-Talk

I used to be down on myself for everything. And I rehearsed negative thoughts about myself over and over in my head for years. But I don't go there anymore. I found it to be the biggest waste of time, and it doesn't get me anywhere. All it does is make me sad and paralyzed, so that my life comes to a halt.

Don't you go there, either. Forget what someone else said to you or about you, or did to you. Don't allow them to have that much control over your life. And don't add to the bruises by saying negative things to yourself all the time. It does no good. It doesn't change anything. Think instead about what God says about you. He says you are wonderfully made and worth dying for. He says He loves you and He created you for a great purpose.

If you are often down on yourself, ask God to show you the good things about you. I know this may seem self-centered, but it's really not. Actually, being negative about yourself all the time is self-centered. Plus, it's exhausting and pointless.

Ask God to give you the proper perspective on yourself and your life. Thank Him for creating you, saving and loving you, and giving you purpose. Ask Him to help you not hinder what He wants to do in your life with any negative self-talk. He doesn't like it. And neither should you. You don't have to live that way.

One of the best ways to stop the negative self-talk is to focus on others and help them in some way. If you are one of those people who can't think of one good thing you could possibly do to help others because of all the things you feel are wrong with you, let me ask, "Can you smile and talk?" Because you have no idea how many people there are in the world whose day could be made and their life changed for the better if someone would just look them in the eye, smile, and say, "Hello."

Everyone needs love, affirmation, and acceptance. People won't care if you're overweight, you have blemishes, your bangs are too short, you're not good at tennis, you flunked biology, you were laid off from your job, you're behind in your mortgage, you haven't been on the front page of a magazine, you're not the smoothest talker in the world, or whatever else you might feel insecure about. They will just care that you smiled at them and let them know that you saw them, you acknowledged their existence, and you accepted and approved of them enough to produce a genuine smile and a warm greeting. If you can do that, don't tell me you do not have a purpose and a ministry. You have no idea how painfully lonely, sad, and afraid people are. I know, because I used to be one of them. You have the power to speak words to others that will bring life to *them* as well as *yourself*. It takes so little effort to speak words that encourage.

The point I am making is don't talk negatively—not to yourself and not to anyone else. Speak the truth from God's Word and God's heart. Speak words of love, kindness, acceptance, and encouragement to others. You can actually communicate all of that in just a few kind words when you have the love of God in your heart.

When talking to yourself, speak words of hope instead of hopelessness. Instead of saying, "You're hopeless," say, "My hope is in the Lord. Thank You, Lord, that You have given me a future and a hope." Speak *God's* truth for you, not your own fear, doubt, criticism, or negativity. I'm not saying you need to play "let's pretend" and never be honest about your feelings. By all means, do not live a life of denial. That doesn't accomplish anything. Nor am I talking about when you are being humorous or joking. You don't have to be legalistic about this. Just be aware of what you are saying and why.

If you have spoken words about yourself that are negative, confess that to the Lord and ask Him to remove those attitudes from you. If you have spoken harsh or wrong words to anyone else, or words that weren't necessarily bad but you know they didn't bring life, confess that before God and ask Him to give you a right heart.

LEARNING HOW TO TALK

In my Bible I have written down in the margin next to one particular passage of Scripture the words "How to Live." Of course, the entire Bible shows us how to live, but if we were to live by these particular seven verses—along with the Ten Commandments—we would be doing well in our everyday lives. These verses could also fit under the title "How to Talk," for they are a perfect guide for speaking words that bring life.

Don't lie, speak the truth. "Putting away lying, let each one of you speak truth with his neighbor, for we are members of one another" (Ephesians 4:25).

Don't let anger influence what you say. "'Be angry, and do not sin': do not let the sun go down on your wrath" (Ephesians 4:26).

Don't give the enemy a place in your heart. "Nor give place to the devil" (Ephesians 4:27).

Speak words that are positive and honest, not shady or fraudulent. "Let no corrupt word proceed out of your mouth, but what is good for necessary edification, that it may impart grace to the hearers" (Ephesians 4:29).

Don't grieve the Holy Spirit in what you say. "Do not grieve the Holy Spirit of God, by whom you were sealed for the day of redemption" (Ephesians 4:30).

Don't speak negative, evil, or bitter words. "Let all bitterness, wrath, anger, clamor, and evil speaking be put away from you, with all malice" (Ephesians 4:31).

Let your speech be Christlike—loving, kind, and forgiving. "Be kind to one another, tenderhearted, forgiving one another, even as God in Christ forgave you" (Ephesians 4:32).

Speak the Word with Boldness

After Peter and John were questioned by the high priest and released, they went to their companions and prayed together that they would all be able to speak with boldness and that God would stretch out His hand to heal and do signs and wonders in the name of Jesus (Acts 4:23-30). After they prayed, "The place where they were assembled together was shaken, and they were all filled with the Holy Spirit and *they spoke the Word of God with boldness*" (Acts 4:31, emphasis added).

God gives us—who believe in His Son—the ability to speak words that are empowered by the Holy Spirit. We, too, can ask God to help us speak the Word of God with boldness.

God spoke the world into being. He gives you the power to speak your world into being too. Pray wherever you are that you will be able to speak words to others that will shake their lives and open them to the influence of the Holy Spirit. May the words you speak bring life not only to you and your situation, but also to all others with whom you have contact. Being able to speak the truth of God with boldness is one of the pillars upon which a life of true success is established.

✣ Prayer Power ✣

God, help me to speak words that lift up and do not tear down, words that compliment instead of criticize, words that speak unconditional love and not human expectations, and words that instill confidence and not uneasiness. Help me to have such faith in Your control in my life that I can "do all things without complaining and disputing" (Philippians 2:14).

Where I have said words that are negative about myself or anyone else, forgive me. Fill me afresh with Your Holy Spirit and pour into my heart Your love, peace, and joy. Help me to treat myself and others with respect, kindness, patience, and love. Help me to always say with conviction that I will not sin with my mouth (Psalm 17:3).

Lord, help me refuse to say negative things about myself. Every time I start to say a critical word, help me to stop immediately and not continue that line of thinking. Teach me to monitor the words I speak to others. Keep me from saying wrong words that may hurt someone or diminish them in any way. Help me not to be careless in this regard.

Teach me to always speak words that are supported by Your truth and glorify You. "Let the words of my mouth and the meditation of my heart be acceptable in Your sight, O Lord, my strength and my Redeemer" (Psalm 19:14).

In Jesus' name I pray.

✦ Word Power ✦

The lips of the righteous know what is acceptable,
but the mouth of the wicked what is perverse.

Proverbs 10:32

There is one who speaks like the piercings of a
sword, but the tongue of the wise promotes health.

Proverbs 12:18

The Lord God has given Me the tongue of
the learned, that I should know how to speak
a word in season to him who is weary.

Isaiah 50:4

Though you probe my heart and examine me at
night, though you test me, you will find nothing;
I have resolved that my mouth will not sin.

Psalm 17:3 niv

I have put My words in your mouth; I have
covered you with the shadow of My hand.

Isaiah 51:16

→ 25 ←

BE HOLY AS GOD IS HOLY

Y ou may be thinking, *Be holy? Me? There is no way I can be holy.*
And you would be absolutely right.

And absolutely wrong.

The truth is, there is no way you can be holy *by yourself.* But God can make you holy. Jesus prepared the way for that to happen when He destroyed the separation between you and God that existed because of sin. Sin is not compatible with the holiness of God.

God said to His people, "You shall be holy, for I the Lord your God am holy" (Leviticus 19:2). But He is not issuing a command to "be holy" the way we say "sit" to a dog. He is extending a gentle invitation to us that says, "Come and be holy like Me." But we can't just say, "I'm going to be holy today" and then we are. Only when we invite God's nature to permeate ours—when we set ourselves apart from the world and align ourselves with Him—can we be holy. We are made holy by being in close contact with the holiness of God.

The more we look to Jesus, the more we become like Him. The more time we spend in the presence of God, the more we take on His attributes. We are *"being transformed into the same image from glory to glory"* (2 Corinthians 3:18, emphasis added). It's something *He* does in us when we live *His* way. It's nothing we can take any credit for, because it's all Him.

Holiness is not an external code or set of rules. A holy person obeys God's rules, but it happens from the inside out. In other words, the Holy Spirit *in* you teaches and guides you, and helps you obey. Otherwise, it would be as if you put oranges on a tree and called it an orange tree. If the vitality of the oranges doesn't come from within, it is not connected to any source of life. That means no real growth.

Receiving Jesus and memorizing Scripture doesn't make you holy. You certainly must do those things, but that is just the beginning. God says to be holy as He is holy. But *we* cannot make ourselves holy. The rules of the Bible don't make us holy. Our own righteousness doesn't accomplish anything. Our righteousness is based on receiving Jesus, who is righteous, and being filled with the Holy Spirit. It is the Holy Spirit *in* us that makes us holy.

Being holy means "to be set apart." That means separating ourselves from anything that is *not* holy. We do that by living in obedience to God and loving Him more than we love anything else. It's recognizing that all the world has to offer is not our source of significance. God is. We are not taken out of the world; we are put into the world. But the world is not our source of life.

As we grow in the Lord, the Holy Spirit becomes a self-corrector inside of us. We are guided by Him, and we find that we do obedient things without even questioning whether we want to anymore. And if we ever think of doing something wrong, we sense an unmistakable pricking of our conscience that is done with scalpel-like precision.

Being holy doesn't mean being perfect. We can never be that. So don't let perfectionism overcome you. Perfectionists are always frustrated because they can't make everything perfect. I know, because I am one of them. We make ourselves miserable seeing all the imperfections in our marriage, in our work, in our life, in the world. We must learn the difference between having order in our life, which we can't function well without, and trying to make things perfect, which will not only drive *us* crazy but *everyone else* around us as well.

The good news is that we are going to especially enjoy heaven, where everything is perfect and in order all the time. But until then we have to come to terms with the fact that we cannot *be* perfect and we cannot *make* things perfect. And we can't judge other people's imperfections. We have to give others the same grace God gives us. This includes our spouse, children, boss, friends, family members, and pastors. We can't expect them to be as perfect as we want ourselves to be.

Being holy is not as easy as it sounds. (Don't worry; I know it doesn't sound easy.) But it is not as impossible as it sounds, either. Because of who you are, God's child, and because of who lives in you, the Holy Spirit, you can be holy. God refers to you as part of a "holy nation" of believers who have been called out of darkness (1 Peter 2:9). You are *called* to separate yourself from all darkness and sin. "As obedient children, not conforming yourselves to the former lusts, as in your ignorance; but as He who called you is holy, you also be holy in all your conduct" (1 Peter 1:14-15). You have to take deliberate steps to clean up your act.

This Is the Way You Clean Your House

Here are some practical things you can do to open your life and heart to the holiness of God.

Ask God to Purify Your Heart

The closer we walk to the Lord, the purer our hearts will be, and the clearer we will see Him. "Blessed are the pure in heart, for they shall see God" (Matthew 5:8).

Get Rid of Any Ties to Another Religion or Faith

God clearly commands that we are not to have any other god but Him. Isaiah speaks of a path we are to walk as believers. And only those who partake of the holiness of God can walk on this path. "A highway shall be there, and a road, and it shall be called the Highway of Holiness. The unclean shall not pass over it, but it shall be for others. Whoever walks the road, although a fool, shall not go astray" (Isaiah 35:8). That means even if we make a dumb mistake, because we are believers in Jesus and have no ties with any other gods, we will be led in safety.

It also says that we shall obtain "joy and gladness" (Isaiah 35:10). This will not happen if we have ties to another religion or faith.

Get Rid of Books or Artifacts Glorifying the Occult or Other Idols

These things have to be destroyed and not given to someone else to compromise and confuse his or her life. Spirits are associated with such items, and you do not want them to be associated with you or anyone else. "Many of those who had practiced magic brought their books together and *burned* them in the sight of all" (Acts 19:19, emphasis added). Ask God to show you anything you need to get rid of.

Separate Yourself from the World

Separating yourself from the world does not mean you can never go to a gas station, grocery store, or restaurant again. It means that the Holy Spirit in you must never be aligned with the spirit of darkness in the world anymore. We must cleanse ourselves of all pollution of our flesh, mind, and spirit and seek to live a holy life (2 Corinthians 7:1). It doesn't mean we never associate with unbelievers. It means we don't allow the world to dictate our thoughts, beliefs, and actions to us.

Pursue Holiness with a Humble Spirit

We cannot dwell with the Lord if we don't have a humble heart. "Thus says the High and Lofty One who inhabits eternity, whose name is Holy: '*I dwell in the high and holy place, with him who has a contrite and humble spirit,* to revive the spirit of the humble, and to revive the heart of the contrite ones'" (Isaiah 57:15, emphasis added). In order to see God, we must desire His holiness. "Pursue peace with all people, and holiness, without which no one will see the Lord" (Hebrews 12:14). We cannot do that without a humble heart.

Worship God Often Every Day

Worship is the direct link to God's holiness. As we worship God—especially for His holiness—we become an open vessel into which God pours His holiness.

When that happens, we are changed by it. The unholiness of the world loses all appeal. "God did not call us to uncleanness, but in holiness" (1 Thessalonians 4:7). Don't forget that we become like what we worship. The more we worship God for His holiness, the more His holiness will permeate our life. We must "give unto the LORD the glory due to His name; worship the LORD *in the beauty of holiness*" (Psalm 29:2, emphasis added). The angels around the throne of God are continually praising Him for His holiness (Isaiah 6:2-3). We must also do that whenever we can.

When a great multitude of enemies came to battle against Jehoshaphat, he and his people fasted and prayed for help from God (2 Chronicles 20:1-4). God told them, "Do not be afraid nor dismayed because of this great multitude, for the battle is not yours, but God's...tomorrow go out against them, for the LORD is with you" (2 Chronicles 20:15-17). Then Jehoshaphat appointed worship singers to go out before the army and "*praise the beauty of holiness*" (2 Chronicles 20:21, emphasis added). As they did that, the enemy was completely defeated. What a great lesson for us.

God loves you so much that He wants to share Himself with you. He even wants to share His holiness, which is the essence of who He is. "No one is holy like the LORD" (1 Samuel 2:2). When you stand in praise, He fills you with His holiness, and it causes you to win the battle against your enemy.

Jesus was holy on earth (Acts 4:29-30). He was *in* the world but not *of* the world. And He is our role model. He devoted Himself entirely to God and wanted only God's will to be done. He died for us—paying the price for our unholiness—and rose again to be victorious over death and hell, and He sent us the Holy Spirit to be an absolute guarantee that we have access to the holiness of God.

Praise God for His holiness, and let it become a reservoir from which you daily draw your own holiness.

✦ Prayer Power ✦

Lord, help me to be holy as You are holy. Jesus, help me to walk as You walked on earth (1 John 2:6). Enable me to be an imitator of You (Ephesians 5:1). Wash over me with Your holiness and cleanse me from the inside out of anything in me that is not holy. Reveal whatever is hidden within me that I need to be rid of—any attitudes, thoughts, or sin that must be gone from my life. Separate me from all that separates me from You, Lord. Help me to get rid of anything in my life that does not glorify You. Give me the conviction and strength I need to step away from whatever is not compatible with Your holiness in me. "Who is like You, glorious in holiness?" (Exodus 15:11). You are mighty and have done great things for me. Holy is Your name (Luke 1:49).

Help me to continually maintain a humble heart of worship before You. Purify my heart and mind so that I can be a partaker of Your holiness (Hebrews 12:10). You are worthy of all praise and honor and glory, for only You are holy.

"O Lord, You are my God. I will exalt You, I will praise Your name, for You have done wonderful things" (Isaiah 25:1). I sing praise to You, Lord, and give thanks at the remembrance of Your holy name (Psalm 30:4). I worship You in the beauty of Your holiness (Psalm 29:2).

In Jesus' name I pray.

✦ Word Power ✦

Having these promises, beloved, let us cleanse ourselves from all filthiness of the flesh and spirit, perfecting holiness in the fear of God.

2 Corinthians 7:1

Who may ascend into the hill of the LORD? Or
who may stand in His holy place? He who has
clean hands and a pure heart, who has not lifted
up his soul to an idol, nor sworn deceitfully.

PSALM 24:3-4

We, being delivered from the hand of our enemies,
might serve Him without fear, in holiness and
righteousness before Him all the days of our life.

LUKE 1:74-75

I speak in human terms because of the weakness
of your flesh. For just as you presented your
members as slaves of uncleanness, and of lawlessness
leading to more lawlessness, so now present your
members as slaves of righteousness for holiness.

ROMANS 6:19

He chose us in Him before the foundation
of the world, that we should be holy and
without blame before Him in love.

EPHESIANS 1:4

26

RECOGNIZE YOUR ENEMY

⸻•⁙•⸻

You have an enemy. And you cannot live in the freedom God has for you if you don't recognize who your enemy is.

Your enemy is the devil. You may have people in your life who act like the devil, and others who appear to you to be the spawn of hell, but they are not your enemy. Satan is. He is the "god of this age" who blinds people to the truth so they can't see the light (2 Corinthians 4:3-4).

You will never be able to enjoy the wholeness God has for you if you accept as truth the lies of the enemy, who wants to rob you. You cannot achieve true success if you are unable to resist the enemy, who is trying to destroy your life. The good news is that you don't have to live with enemy attacks because God is greater than anything the enemy can manifest in opposition to you. God is on your side (Psalm 118:6). I ask you, if *God* is *for* you, who can possibly succeed against you (Romans 8:31)?

You may be thinking that you don't want to have any dealings with the devil. But you will, whether you want to or not. Just as God has a plan for your life, the enemy has a plan for you as well. You want the plans of God for your life to succeed and the plans of the enemy to fail. This requires understanding God's will and living in it as well as knowing who your enemy is and what his plans are. Jesus said, "The thief does not come except to steal, and to kill, and to destroy. I have come that they may have life, and that they may have it more abundantly" (John 10:10). That tells you all you need to know about *who* is planning *what* for you.

God has given you a number of weapons to fight the enemy and armor to wear as protection. You must learn to "put on the whole armor of God, that you may be able to stand against the wiles of the devil. For we do not wrestle against flesh and blood, but against principalities, against powers, against the rulers of the darkness of this age, against spiritual hosts of wickedness in the heavenly places" (Ephesians 6:11-12). If you put on the whole armor of God, you can withstand whatever the enemy sends your way (Ephesians 6:13).

The armor of God is not something we put on and then go hide under the bed. We put it on not only for defensive purposes but offensive purposes as well. While it's true that our battle with the enemy has already been won—because of what Jesus accomplished on the cross—that doesn't mean we do nothing. We have to exhibit strong faith in God and His Word, and we have to pray aggressively without backing down.

Pharaoh chased after the Israelites when they left Egypt. As he and his enormous army approached them at the edge of the Red Sea, the Israelites were terrified of their enemy and cried out to God. They asked Moses why he had led them there to die in the wilderness. He told them, "Do not be afraid. Stand still, and see the salvation of the LORD, which He will accomplish for you today. For the Egyptians whom you see today, you shall see again no more forever. The LORD will fight for you, and you shall hold your peace" (Exodus 14:13-14).

God will fight for *us* against our enemy too. But He doesn't expect us to do nothing. The Israelites had to *believe* God. And so do *we*. They had to step out onto the sea floor with a wall of water on either side of them and walk across to the other side. What faith that must have required. God will make a way for us as well, but we also must step out in faith and do what He tells us to do. We have to use the spiritual weapons He has given us of His Word, prayer, and worship. We must be in the right place at the right time—which means being in the protective covering of His will.

Resist the Enemy with the Word of God

The Word of God is your most powerful weapon against the enemy. In describing the armor of God, His Word is referred to as "the sword of the Spirit" (Ephesians 6:17). It cuts through everything. If you don't know God's truth, you cannot discern the enemy's lies. The enemy will steal away the Word of God from anyone who is not solid in the knowledge of it (Mark 4:15). Read Ephesians 6:10-18 in your Bible often so that you always understand the armor God has given you. Never tire of reading God's Word, knowing that the enemy never tires of doing evil (1 Peter 5:8).

Resist the Enemy with Prayer

If the Word of God is our weapon, prayer is the way we do battle. Prayer is also part of your armor. Praying is the actual fight itself. Don't let the enemy keep you struggling with sickness, injury, misery, one disaster after another, problems with children, strife in your marriage, financial struggles, and constant threats to your well-being or your life. God has given you authority in prayer.

Use the authority given you in Jesus' name. "Behold, I give you the authority to trample on serpents and scorpions, and *over all the power of the enemy,* and nothing shall by any means hurt you" (Luke 10:19, emphasis added). If you are facing enemy assault, declare the truth and promises of God in your prayers. Pray about what is happening and thank God that He will guard you from the evil one (2 Thessalonians 3:3).

When the situation is serious, *fast* and pray. The enemy cannot continue to oppose you for long when you do. That's because fasting and prayer are powerful to set you free from the threats of evil. (More about this in chapter 27, "Fast and Pray to Win.")

Resist the Enemy with Worship

One of the most powerful weapons against the enemy is worship. Worship is a weapon of warfare because it welcomes the presence of God. The enemy cannot stay in God's presence. He hates it. It reminds him of when he gave up his job as worship leader in heaven because he wanted to exalt himself and be like God. His fall was great, and he knows he is defeated, but he is counting on people like you and me to be ignorant of that.

I have been attacked countless times by the enemy in the areas of my health, mind, marriage, children, emotions, work, and on and on. Each time that happens, I ask God to show me everything I need to know about what is happening. I declare God's Word, and then I worship God in *every way* and for *everything* I can think of. I praise Him for who He is and all He has done. Each time, worship and praise broke the stronghold the enemy was trying to erect in my life. "I will call upon the LORD, *who is worthy* to be praised; so shall I be saved from my enemies" (Psalm 18:3, emphasis added).

Resist the Enemy by Staying in God's Will

It is a powerful thing to submit your life to God and live in obedience to His ways. "Submit to God. Resist the devil and he will flee from you" (James 4:7). If the enemy attacks you, ask the Lord to show you any place in your life where you are not walking in obedience to God's ways or His will. Remember that all His ways are for your benefit (Psalm 19:9).

That being said, if you are living in obedience to the best of your ability and are in the will of God to the best of your knowledge, don't let the enemy cause you to blame yourself for what *he* is doing. Pouring on guilt and condemnation is one of his favorite ploys, and he will dump on as much as you will accept.

Keep in mind that when you are walking with God and living His way, you are on the side that wins. The enemy ultimately loses (John 12:31). Of course, if you walk outside of God's will, you come out from under the covering of His protection and give the enemy an entry point. If that happens, remember whose side *you're* on and get back into proper alignment with God.

Ask God to Show You What Is Really Going On

When something unsettling is happening and you aren't sure exactly what is going on, ask God to show you if it is part of *His* plan for your life or if this is an attack by the enemy. Don't be too quick to blame yourself, your spouse, your boss, or your neighbor. It may be entirely coming from the enemy's camp. Pray for your eyes to be opened to the truth. Ask God to help you discern what you're facing.

The better you know God and His Word, and the closer you walk with Him, the quicker you will be able to spot a counterfeit and identify the enemy. God is not going to bring something bad into your life (Psalm 25:8). He will never destroy you, bring problems, or cause strife between you and your spouse. That's the work of the enemy.

You must also learn to discern between *spiritual* opposition and *human* opposition. Although the enemy exists in the spirit realm, he can manifest through anyone who will believe his lies. Human opposition happens because people ignorantly allow themselves to become a tool of the enemy. If we don't understand that, we could be wasting our time struggling against a person or a number of people instead of warring against the enemy as we should.

If you are having tremendous opposition from another person, go to war in the spirit realm. Often the battle can be settled there. I have found this especially true in marriage. If married couples who are fighting would realize how often it is the enemy who is inspiring the actions and words of one or both partners, they would see how they are being used as his pawns. God wants your marriage to be good; the enemy wants it destroyed. "Though we walk in the flesh, we do not war according to the flesh. For the weapons of our warfare are not carnal but mighty in God for pulling down strongholds" (2 Corinthians 10:3-4).

God said to Jeremiah, "Call to Me and I will answer you, and show you great and mighty things, which you do not know" (Jeremiah 33:3).

We all need that kind of insight into the spirit realm in order to understand what we are facing and the degree of strength the Lord mounts on our behalf. In order to pray with the greatest effectiveness, ask God what you need to know, so you can have a sense of *what* you are praying about, and *how* He wants you to pray.

Jesus came to defeat the enemy, and He did. "For this purpose the Son of God was manifested, that He might destroy the works of the devil" (1 John 3:8). Because He is your Savior, you don't need to live in fear of what the enemy will try to do to you. Just stay close to God and rely on His power on your behalf. He promises, "I will never leave you nor forsake you" (Hebrews 13:5). But always keep your weapons ready.

⇢ Prayer Power ⇠

Lord, I thank You that You have delivered me from my enemy. Thank You, Jesus, that You came to "destroy the works of the devil" and You have already won the battle (1 John 3:8). Help me not to be deceived by the deceiver. Open my eyes to the truth so that I can identify his lies. I know that "though I walk in the midst of trouble, You will revive me; You will stretch out Your hand against the wrath of my enemies, and Your right hand will save me" (Psalm 138:7).

Help me to "be wise in what is good, and simple concerning evil" for I know that You, the God of peace, "will crush Satan" under my feet quickly (Romans 16:19-20). Help me to "take up the whole armor of God," so that I can stand strong during enemy attack (Ephesians 6:13).

Lord, keep me aware of when the enemy is attacking. Help me to be strong in Your Word and continuously in prayer so that I will not be caught off guard. Help me to never "give place to the devil" with disobedience to Your ways (Ephesians 4:27). Help me instead to submit to You and resist the devil so that he will flee from me (James 4:7). Enable me to stay in Your will so that I never come out from under the umbrella of Your protection. Teach me to make worship of You my first reaction to enemy attack. I praise You, Lord, for You have "delivered me out of all trouble; and my eye has seen its desire upon my enemies" (Psalm 54:7).

In Jesus' name I pray.

⇸ WORD POWER ⇷

Be sober, be vigilant; because your adversary
the devil walks about like a roaring lion,
seeking whom he may devour.

1 PETER 5:8

Do not rejoice over me, my enemy; when
I fall, I will arise; when I sit in darkness,
the LORD will be a light to me.

MICAH 7:8

Let the redeemed of the LORD say so, whom He
has redeemed from the hand of the enemy.

PSALM 107:2

"Not by might nor by power, but by My
Spirit," says the LORD of hosts.

ZECHARIAH 4:6

You who love the LORD, hate evil! He
preserves the souls of His saints; He delivers
them out of the hand of the wicked.

PSALM 97:10

27

FAST AND PRAY TO WIN

Fasting and praying to the Lord is one of the most powerful things you can ever do. I believe it is such an important spiritual discipline that I don't see how you will experience total freedom, complete wholeness, and true success without it.

Fasting is deliberately not eating food for a specific time so you can turn your back on what your flesh wants most and position God as everything. Fasting brings you into a greater knowledge of the Lord and releases a more powerful work of the Holy Spirit in your life.

More than 25 great reasons to fast can be found in Isaiah 58, and any one of them would be reason enough to engage in this spiritual discipline. In just verse 6 alone, there are four great reasons:

1. *"To loose the bonds of wickedness."* Anytime evil has a hold on you, fasting releases you and works freedom *in* your life. It's as if the Holy Spirit pours anointing oil on you and the enemy can't hang on. Through fasting and prayer, you will find greater and speedier freedom.

2. *"To undo the heavy burdens."* Fasting is the way to get free of any burden you have. Every day there can be burdens on you that your shoulders were not created to carry. Fasting, with prayer, is the best way to see those lifted.

3. *"To let the oppressed go free."* Deliverance happens when you

fast. Even if it doesn't happen *during* the fast itself, fasting and prayer pave the way for it.

4. *"That you break every yoke?"* Breaking the yoke means freedom from any kind of restriction, whether put on you by the enemy, others, or your own limited understanding of what freedom in Christ really is. There is a question mark at the end of this sentence because this entire verse is a question. God is asking, "Isn't this what I, the Lord, want to see happen when you fast?"

God is saying that He doesn't want us to fast just to make our voices heard, but rather to humble ourselves before Him so He can accomplish these things in our lives (Isaiah 58:4-5). "'Now, therefore,' says the LORD, 'turn to Me with all your heart, with fasting, with weeping, and with mourning'" (Joel 2:12).

Fasting has been one of the most powerful spiritual tools in my life. I have never fasted and prayed and not had some kind of breakthrough—either in my own life or in the lives of those for whom I prayed. Jesus said there were certain spiritual bondages that could only be eliminated by fasting (Mark 9:29). I believe that was an extremely important aspect of my deliverance. All four of the reasons for fasting I listed above from Isaiah 58:6 describe exactly what happened to me in an undeniable way. Since that time periodic fasting has affected every area of my physical, mental, emotional, and spiritual being. It will do the same for you.

When you want to break down any plan of evil that is trying to erect a stronghold in your life, or you want to have a burden lifted off your shoulders, or you need freedom and breakthrough—not only in your life but also in the lives of those you care about—fasting and prayer will do all that.

Fasting Is a Step of Obedience

Fasting must be done along with prayer, otherwise you are just on a very strict diet. You deny yourself food for a specific period of time so that you can devote yourself to prayer and focusing on God. Just as the Bible is not simply a history book, fasting is not simply an ancient practice we look back on and thank God we don't have to do today. It is every bit as relevant and crucial for a life of true success as it ever was. Jesus said, "*When* you fast" (Matthew 6:16, emphasis added). He did *not* say, "*If* you *might someday feel* like fasting."

God knows that the greatest pleasure for all of us is eating. None of us ever *wants* to stop eating and deny ourselves, but when we do that as a step of obedience to God for His glory, we tell our body who is in charge. Fasting will break the hold of the enemy on your life so you can get free from whatever binds you. For example, bad health habits, obsessive thought processes, or negative emotions can all be broken through fasting and prayer. That has been my personal experience.

Fasting helps you increase in spiritual strength, cleanses your heart, and gives you clarity. You can receive revelation from God that will give you the knowledge you need or solutions to specific problems. As you grow closer to God, you can hear Him speaking to your heart about direction for your life. Or you may be able to see a way through a difficult situation. "We fasted and entreated our God for this, and He answered our prayer" (Ezra 8:23).

When you need to resist sin and temptation of any kind, fasting and prayer will break the hold that enticement has on you. When your life seems out of control, fasting and prayer will bring it back under God's control and take away confusion. As you fast and pray—or after the fast is over—you will sense God's power flowing more mightily through you. Fasting with prayer is a gift and a privilege from God, and it will positively affect every aspect of your life. You may not always *want* to engage in fasting, but every time you do, you'll be so glad you did because of the amazing breakthrough you'll experience.

What to Do on a Short Fast

For the purposes of this book, I am just talking about a short fast of only 20 to 36 hours periodically. If the Lord calls you to a longer fast, read one of the many good books out on fasting to see how to approach it and be successful on it.

Pray about your fast first. Ask God how long it should be. Ask the Holy Spirit to lead you as you pray and fast so that you are taking advantage of this time to pray about things you might not have thought to pray about otherwise. "If you are led by the Spirit, you are not under the law" (Galatians 5:18).

If you are just starting to fast, begin with fasting only one meal. Use that time to pray. Don't be impatient for results. Don't say, "I have been fasting for 45 minutes, and I still don't feel as though any satanic stronghold of evil has been broken in my life." Please, give God time. You may notice nothing at all during the fast and only begin to see some of the results in the days or weeks following.

As you are fasting, drink plenty of pure, clean water. If you feel weak, prepare a vegetable broth. Put an onion, a potato, two carrots, and two stalks of celery (all cleaned, peeled, and quartered) in a pan of one or two quarts of pure water. Let it simmer for an hour before drinking the broth. You need a certain amount of health and strength to fast, and the broth will help you. Eventually, you won't need it.

God knows what you are able to do, so do what you can. If you can only fast one meal a week as you drink vegetable broth, then do that. The point is to deny yourself what your *flesh* wants in order to do what *God* wants. "Oh, taste and see that the LORD is good; blessed is the man who trusts in Him!" (Psalm 34:8).

Every time you fast, read Isaiah 58:6-14. I have included it at the end of this chapter. In it God describes the kind of fast He wants and what He intends to accomplish through it. It will remind you of why you're fasting in the first place, and what you should do as you fast. These verses tell you what your rewards will be. For example, "Your healing shall spring forth speedily." "You shall call, and the LORD will answer." He "will guide you continually," "satisfy your soul," "strengthen your bones," and much more (Isaiah 58:8-11). Every time I read this section of Scripture, I am inspired all over again in even greater depths. I know you will be too.

If everything needing to be accomplished in our lives could be done without fasting, then why did Jesus fast? Surely if anyone would not have needed to fast, it would have been Him. But He knew that fasting was the only way to see certain things happen. After Jesus came back from His 40-day fast, His healing and miracle ministry began. If Jesus had to fast, how much more do we in order to move into powerful ministry?

Fasting prepares you for a new touch of God on your life. Many great people of the Bible fasted just before a great breakthrough. It will be the same for you. Are you due for a breakthrough?

✢ Prayer Power ✦

Lord, I pray You would help me to fast and pray to Your glory. Enable me to put aside my favorite activity—eating the food You have provided for me—in favor of exalting You as everything in my life. Show me how often and how long I should fast, and enable me to accomplish it. Help me to be well enough and strong enough to fast in the way You want me to.

Thank You that when I fast, You will break down the strongholds of the enemy in my life and loose all bonds of wickedness. I pray You will break any wrong thinking or obsessions in me. Release me from the heavy burdens I have been carrying. Break every yoke of bondage in my life. Show me whom and what to pray for as I fast. Reveal ways to pray I don't yet understand.

Help me to do what I can to help others and feed the hungry. Show me where I should extend myself to those who are afflicted or suffering. Help me to honor the Sabbath—Your holy day—by doing what honors You and not going my own way and doing what I want. Help me to want what *You* want.

Thank You that as I fast, You will look after the details of my life and give me direction. Thank You that my "light shall break forth like the morning" and my "healing shall spring forth speedily" (Isaiah 58:8). Thank You that when I call, You will answer (Isaiah 58:9).

In Jesus' name I pray.

✦ WORD POWER ✦

Is this not the fast that I have chosen: to loose the
bonds of wickedness, to undo the heavy burdens, to
let the oppressed go free, and that you break every
yoke? Is it not to share your bread with the hungry,
and that you bring to your house the poor who are
cast out; when you see the naked, that you cover
him, and not hide yourself from your own flesh?

Then your light shall break forth like the morning,
your healing shall spring forth speedily, and
your righteousness shall go before you; the
glory of the LORD shall be your rear guard. Then
you shall call, and the LORD will answer; you
shall cry, and He will say, "Here I am."

If you take away the yoke from your midst, the
pointing of the finger, and speaking wickedness,
if you extend your soul to the hungry and satisfy
the afflicted soul, then your light shall dawn in
the darkness, and your darkness shall be as the
noonday. The LORD will guide you continually,
and satisfy your soul in drought, and strengthen
your bones; you shall be like a watered garden, and
like a spring of water, whose waters do not fail.

Those from among you shall build the old waste
places; you shall raise up the foundations of many
generations; and you shall be called the Repairer
of the Breach, the Restorer of Streets to Dwell
In…The mouth of the Lord has spoken.

ISAIAH 58:6-14

✣ 28 ✤

STAND STRONG
IN TOUGH TIMES

———◆◆◆———

The most trying situations we face have to do with sickness, injury, financial problems, marital strife, relational difficulties, work-related challenges, and, the worst, the passing of someone you love or facing your own impending death. We need to know that God is with us during these terribly upsetting times. We have to be sure that we can stand strong, no matter what is happening.

In my book *Just Enough Light for the Step I'm On,* I talk about how we must learn to walk with God in total trust—even in the darkest times of our lives. God requires that the first step be ours toward Him. We must reach up to Him and say, "Lord, I depend on You. Lead me in the way I should go." When we do that, He will set us on the correct path, point us in the right direction, and smooth out the crooked places. He will get us moving and keep us from going around in circles so that we don't come back again and again to the same problems. Then, as we take one step at a time, holding on to God's hand, He leads us where we need to go.

The problem is that we often forget to hold on to God's hand and depend on Him for every step we take. We think that if God will just get us over this hump, we can handle it from here. But one of the reasons God allows us to go through difficult situations is so that we *will* learn to depend on Him. When we do, we are better able to stand strong in tough times.

We tend to think that if we depend on God, it's a sign of weakness on our part. And that's true! But that's the *good news*. When we recognize that we don't have what it takes to get where we need to go, but *God* does, then we are beginning to understand true freedom. When we walk with God, He will get us through anything.

The most amazing thing is that when we walk close to God, even our most difficult times have an aspect of good. Some situations may be so horrendous that the only good we see are the moments we cling to God and we have a deep sense of His presence. But those are precious moments. The key is to look for God in the situation. No matter how dark things get, God will give us the light we need for the step we're on. He will supply what we must have for the moment we're in.

How to Stand Strong in Tough Times

God teaches us how to walk with Him—depending on Him for every step. He also teaches us how to stand strong when challenges arise that threaten to blow us away. Here are some reliable ways to stand strong in tough times.

Stand in what you know is true of the Lord. "We must give the more earnest heed to the things we have heard, lest we drift away" (Hebrews 2:1).

Stand on God's Word. "Princes persecute me without a cause, but my heart stands in awe of Your word" (Psalm 119:161).

Stand in obedience to God. "The righteous will come through trouble" (Proverbs 12:13).

Stand knowing you could fall. "Let him who thinks he stands take heed lest he fall" (1 Corinthians 10:12).

Stand by being in God's will. "Epaphras, who is one of you... greets you, always laboring fervently for you in prayers, that you may stand perfect and complete in all the will of God" (Colossians 4:12).

Stand by giving yourself away. "A generous man devises generous things, and by generosity he shall stand" (Isaiah 32:8).

Stand away from evil. "When the storm has swept by, the wicked are gone, but the righteous stand firm forever" (Proverbs 10:25 NIV).

Stand in the traditions you know are of the Lord. "Stand fast and hold the traditions which you were taught, whether by word or our epistle" (2 Thessalonians 2:15).

Stand courageous in your faith. "Watch, stand fast in the faith, be brave, be strong. Let all that you do be done with love" (1 Corinthians 16:13-14).

Stand making sure your house is not divided. "If a house is divided against itself, that house cannot stand" (Mark 3:25).

Stand in the counsel of God and what He has spoken to your heart. "My counsel shall stand, and I will do all My pleasure" (Isaiah 46:10).

Conquering the Storms of Life

When you find yourself in the middle of a storm, ask God, "Am I in this storm because I have done something wrong?" "Is this an attack of the enemy?" Or, "Is it because I am in Your will and You are using this for Your purpose?" The answer you discern in your heart will help you to gain a clearer picture of what is really happening.

If a storm is raging in your life, pray and read the Bible more. Stand strong in your faith. Look around for others who are suffering too and pray for them. Don't become discouraged when it seems there is no hope. God can make a way in the wilderness.

God opened up the Red Sea and made a way for the Israelites to cross over it on dry land. He led them in the daytime by a cloud—even in the desert there was a cloud for shade—and at night there was fire for light. When they had no water, He "brought streams out of the rock, and caused waters to run down like rivers" (Psalm 78:12-16). He provided what they needed when it seemed there was no way to get it. He brought them abundance in the wilderness where there was none.

When God brought water from the rocks for the people to drink, I am sure it was better, purer, and more refreshing than any water they had ever had. He also caused manna to miraculously appear so they would have food to eat. It was so perfect that it sustained those people for 40 years in good health.

God can provide for you too. In the dry, parched areas of your life—even the parts that are wilting and wasting and where there seems to be no hope—God can split the hard areas open and bring forth streams of pure refreshment in the wasteland. You will see how the wilderness can be a place of blessing for you if you don't rebel against God when He allows you to go through it.

Unfortunately, the Israelites didn't do that. They turned against God and complained instead of thanking Him for their provision. "They sinned even more against Him by rebelling against the Most High in the wilderness" (Psalm 78:17). They weren't grateful. They didn't see the blessings that were in front of them. They spoke against God by questioning whether He would ever provide for them well enough (Psalm 78:18-20). They insolently said something to the effect of, "Yes, God brought water out of a rock, but can He feed us what we want?" We insult God when we doubt that He can meet our needs. Instead of questioning God in the wilderness, we must thank Him for His provision there. Blaming Him for things that happened is an exercise in futility. He is the only one who can walk us through it or lift us out of it. And He is the only one who can provide what we need while we're in it.

We all have times of doubt just as the Israelites did. Perhaps we don't doubt that God *can,* but we doubt that He *will.* Or we doubt that He *wants* to. Or we doubt that He *cares.* Or we doubt we are worthy of

His help. But doubt means we are doubting who *He is* and what His Word says.

The Purpose of Suffering

In life there is suffering. We all suffer at times. Jesus went through more suffering than any of us will ever know. He was beaten, tortured, nailed to a cross, separated from God, descended into hell, and bore all sin of the world on Himself. And He had the scars to prove it. Through it all, He obeyed God perfectly.

I would never compare our suffering to that of Jesus, but having scars to prove you've suffered can give you credibility with people. Because of what you have come through, you have a more penetrating voice into the life of someone going through the same situation. Your suffering can be the very thing that saves someone else from the brink of destruction.

What helped me to have greater peace about my own suffering is that it has been a help to others. If I can help someone get through their pain and suffering, then that is redemption for both of us. I am not saying that God brings suffering on us deliberately. I am saying that He uses the difficult things that happen to us for His glory. He will do all that for you in your time of suffering too. In the Lord, there is a great purpose in hard times, even when you cannot yet see it.

When going through hard times, take your eyes off your circumstances and put them on the Lord and His Word. Believe His truth *above* whatever you are experiencing. That does not mean denying your circumstances; it means believing that God's Word triumphs over all. Don't focus on what you see; focus on God's promises. Remember that Jesus said, "The things which are impossible with men are possible with God" (Luke 18:27).

We are fragile and breakable—but that is the point. In our weak state, we are the instrument God uses for His purposes. That way, when we stand strong in tough times, we know it is because of His power and not our own doing. We cannot take credit, but must give all the glory to God.

⇒ Prayer Power ⇐

Lord, I pray You would help me to stand strong in all I know of You. Teach me to stand on Your Word, no matter what is happening in my life. Enable me to stand away from sin and evil, and be strong in obedience to Your ways. I acknowledge that I am weak, but I rejoice that You are strong in me—especially during times of trial and difficulty. Help me to learn what I need to know from each challenge I face. Lead me on the path You have for me. I don't want to take a single step without You.

Help me in the situation I am facing now. Lift me out of any hopelessness, fear, doubt, or frustration. Enable me to be firm in faith and always in Your will. Thank You for helping me stand strong in the face of enemy opposition. I am grateful You have armed me with strength for the battle (Psalm 18:39).

So many times "I would have lost heart, unless I had believed that I would see the goodness of the LORD in the land of the living" (Psalm 27:13). Enable me to see Your truth in every situation (Psalm 119:18). Help me to become so strong in You that I can stand without wavering, no matter what happens. Teach me to rest in You, knowing that You will give me what I need for the moment I am in. I am determined to "count it all joy" when I go through trials, because of the perfecting work You will do for me (James 1:2-4). "Though I walk in the midst of trouble, You will revive me" (Psalm 138:7).

In Jesus' name I pray.

↠ WORD POWER ↞

Beloved, do not think it strange concerning the fiery trial which is to try you, as though some strange thing happened to you; but rejoice to the extent that you partake of Christ's sufferings, that when His glory is revealed, you may also be glad with exceeding joy.

1 PETER 4:12-13

My brethren, count it all joy when you fall into various trials, knowing that the testing of your faith produces patience. But let patience have its perfect work, that you may be perfect and complete, lacking nothing.

JAMES 1:2-4

We are hard-pressed on every side, yet not crushed; we are perplexed, but not in despair; persecuted, but not forsaken; struck down, but not destroyed—always carrying about in the body the dying of the Lord Jesus, that the life of Jesus also may be manifested in our body.

2 CORINTHIANS 4:8-10

Our light affliction, which is but for a moment, is working for us a far more exceeding and eternal weight of glory, while we do not look at the things which are seen, but at the things which are not seen. For the things which are seen are temporary, but the things which are not seen are eternal.

2 CORINTHIANS 4:17-18

He said to me, "My grace is sufficient for you, for My strength is made perfect in weakness." Therefore most gladly I will rather boast in my infirmities, that the power of Christ may rest upon me. Therefore I take pleasure in infirmities, in reproaches, in needs, in persecutions, in distresses, for Christ's sake. For when I am weak, then I am strong.

2 CORINTHIANS 12:9-10

MOVE IN THE
POWER OF GOD

———◦•◦•◦———

The only way we can live in freedom, wholeness, and true success is by the power of God. It's impossible otherwise.

The Bible says the "message of the cross...is the power of God" (1 Corinthians 1:18). The power of God is exemplified in Jesus and what He did on the cross. And it is manifested in our lives by the Holy Spirit *in* us.

Paul said he didn't come to people to impress them with his speaking skills, or to draw attention to himself so they would admire *him*. He wanted to show them a demonstration of the Holy Spirit. "My speech and my preaching were not with persuasive words of human wisdom, *but in demonstration of the Spirit and of power, that your faith should not be in the wisdom of men but in the power of God*" (1 Corinthians 2:4-5, emphasis added).

That's what we want too. We want to depend on God to do in our lives what needs to be done so that our faith is not in our own efforts, but in His power. We don't worship God's power; we worship *God*, and have faith *in Him* and His power on our behalf.

Paul was "caught up into Paradise" and given a life-changing vision of the highest heaven, which is the presence of God (2 Corinthians

12:4). To keep Paul from any pride—and others from any adulation over Paul because of his grand experience—God allowed Satan to give him "a thorn in the flesh." Paul "pleaded with the Lord three times that it might depart" from him. But God said to him, *"My grace is sufficient for you, for My strength is made perfect in weakness."* Paul said in light of that, "Therefore most gladly I will rather boast in my infirmities, that the power of Christ may rest upon me" (2 Corinthians 12:7-9, emphasis added). The power of Christ on Paul was the presence of the Holy Spirit, who enabled him to do all God had called him to do. Paul was grateful that his weakness allowed God's power to manifest in him.

What does this mean for you and me? It means that sometimes God allows things to happen to us so that we are made certain that it is not our human effort that will accomplish what needs to happen, but it will only be done *by the power of God.* God's grace will get us through, and *God's strength will be shown perfect in our weakness.* Paul said he would rather be weak so the power of God would rest on him. I agree. We can do far more by the power of God than we can ever do on our own.

It is important to understand this, especially in times when our personal weakness is on full display in such a way that we cannot deny it. From our perspective, it is painful. But from *God's* perspective, it is good. When we are unmistakably weak, God's power can be unmistakably seen.

Moving in the Power of God

God existed before all creation. He created the heavens and the earth without anything preexisting. "He has made the earth by His power; He has established the world by His wisdom, and stretched out the heaven by His understanding" (Jeremiah 51:15). He doesn't need anything from which to create something.

When the "earth was without form, and void; and darkness was on the face of the deep" then "the Spirit of God was hovering over the face of the waters" (Genesis 1:2). Hovering implies movement. This movement of the Holy Spirit has significance for you. Although the Holy Spirit resides in you, He is always moving. He doesn't move in and out of your life; He is always *working* in your life. He is described in the Bible as water (John 7:37-39), as a dove (Matthew 3:16), as fire (Acts 2:3-4), and as oil (1 John 2:20). None of these is stationary. Their very nature is to be moving. Just as these descriptions of Him involve movement, the Holy Spirit is always moving in your life. He is active, whether you are at the moment or not.

Because the Holy Spirit is not stationary, He won't let you be stationary for long. He will not let you stop growing until your spirit is fully aligned with God's. God wants you to be *inspired* by the Holy Spirit, *ignited* by the Holy Spirit, *enabled* by the Holy Spirit, and *empowered* by the Holy Spirit. That means you will always be active in your spirit.

Don't Forget Your Source of Power

We can never forget where our power comes from, especially in times when we feel powerless. The Bible says of the Israelites, "How often they provoked Him in the wilderness, and grieved Him in the desert! Yes, again and again they tempted God, and limited the Holy One of Israel. *They did not remember His power:* The day when He redeemed them from the enemy" (Psalm 78:40-42, emphasis added).

We cannot let that happen to us. The Israelites forgot God and lived their own way, and as a result, limited what God could do in their lives. They didn't remember His power to redeem them from the enemy. They didn't move in the power of God, so they ended up wandering around in the wilderness for 40 years.

We often do the same thing. When the enemy is attacking us or disaster happens—in our health, finances, relationships, emotions, mind, family, and more—we become afraid. We are shaken. We try to fix the situation ourselves. We attempt to take control of it instead of inviting the Holy Spirit to lift us above the obstacles or usher us through the rough terrain ahead of us. What we must do instead is trust that God knows where we need to go and He knows how to get us there. We have to release our grip on all we cling to and submit to the power of God working on our behalf. *We must never forget God's power.*

God empowers the weak, so they can excel by His power and according to His will. "Those who wait on the LORD shall renew their strength; they shall mount up with wings like eagles, they shall run and not be weary, they shall walk and not faint" (Isaiah 40:31). That describes what happens to us when we recognize our weaknesses and depend on the power of God.

The Manifestation of God's Power

Next to God's creation of the world, is there any greater manifestation of God's power than the resurrection of Jesus? He was publicly crucified and buried, and yet He was clearly missing from a sealed tomb and then appeared to many of His followers as the resurrected Lord. What kind of power can accomplish that? Only the power of God. That same resurrection power is in *you.*

Jesus was crucified in weakness, and yet He lives by the power of God. It is the same for you in that you are weak, but you live—both here and for eternity—by the power of God (2 Corinthians 13:4). "God both raised up the Lord and will also raise us up by His power" (1 Corinthians 6:14). Jesus wasn't resurrected from the dead so you could live a happy life. He was resurrected to save you from death and hell so that you can live a life of *power.*

God doesn't want you to live a life without power. He wants to empower you to live the life He has for you.

Because God is all-powerful, it means that "with God all things are possible" (Mark 10:27). God "gives life to the dead and calls those things which do not exist as though they did" (Romans 4:17). That means God is able to create something from nothing and bring to life something that was dead. We desperately want that in our lives. God has all the power we need and He doesn't want us to ever doubt that. He doesn't want us to be "headstrong, haughty, lovers of pleasure rather than lovers of God, *having a form of godliness by denying its power*" (2 Timothy 3:4-5, emphasis added). We want to be a submitted and humble lover of God who lives God's way by the power of His Spirit.

Even though you may not yet see how your problems will ever be solved, God sees it. While you may be overwhelmed by your circumstances, God is never overwhelmed. You have to trust Him and His power on your behalf. He wants to see His power released into your life. Work *with* Him on this. Ask Him every day to empower you to live the life He has for you.

⇢ PRAYER POWER ⇠

Lord, I am grateful for Your power extended to me. You have shown Yourself strong on my behalf countless times because my heart is loyal to You (2 Chronicles 16:9). By Your great and almighty power You have saved and redeemed me (Nehemiah 1:10). You have delivered me, protected me, and provided for me, and I know You will continue to do so.

All power belongs to You, Lord (Psalm 62:11). You uphold all things by the word of Your power (Hebrews 1:3). Thank You that because You are all-powerful, that means all things are possible. Therefore I refuse to become discouraged or fearful about any aspect of my life. I will not trust in the wisdom of man, but I will trust in You and Your perfect wisdom and power.

Lord, You give power to the weak and increase their strength. I thank You that I am the beneficiary of that. Help me to never forget Your power to redeem, save, restore, and renew. No matter what happens, I want to turn to You first and move in the power of Your Spirit.

"Be exalted, O LORD, in Your own strength!" I will "sing and praise Your power" (Psalm 21:13). God of hope, help me to "abound in hope by the power of the Holy Spirit" (Romans 15:13). "For Yours is the power and the glory forever" (Matthew 6:13).

In Jesus' name I pray.

✦ WORD POWER ✦

The eyes of the LORD run to and fro throughout
the whole earth, to show Himself strong on
behalf of those whose heart is loyal to Him.

2 CHRONICLES 16:9

Have you not known? Have you not heard? The
everlasting God, the LORD, the Creator of the ends of
the earth, neither faints nor is weary. His understanding
is unsearchable. He gives power to the weak, and to
those who have no might He increases strength.

ISAIAH 40:28-29

Yours, O LORD, is the greatness, the power and the
glory, the victory and the majesty; for all that is in
heaven and in earth is Yours; Yours is the kingdom,
O LORD, and You are exalted as head over all.

1 CHRONICLES 29:11

What is the exceeding greatness of His power
toward us who believe, according to the working
of His mighty power which He worked in Christ
when He raised Him from the dead and seated
Him at His right hand in the heavenly places.

EPHESIANS 1:19-20

God, You are more awesome than Your holy
places. The God of Israel is He who gives
strength and power to His people.

PSALM 68:35

✦ 30 ✦

REFUSE TO GIVE UP

———

Problems are a part of life. That's because we live in an imperfect world. But the good news is that we serve a perfect God who gives us abundant hope. I say to you as Paul said, "May the God of hope fill you with all joy and peace in believing, *that you may abound in hope by the power of the Holy Spirit*" (Romans 15:13, emphasis added).

Hope happens by the power of the Holy Spirit.

God says that the future He has for you is filled with hope and peace. "I know the thoughts that I think toward you, says the LORD, thoughts of *peace* and not of evil, to give you a *future* and a *hope*" (Jeremiah 29:11, emphasis added). God wants *you* to think about your hope-filled future too. That's because He doesn't want you to ever give up—not on Him, not on yourself, not on your life.

Too often, in the time we're waiting for God to answer our prayers and move on our behalf, we become discouraged and lose hope. In order to keep that from happening, there are certain things we can do.

We can stay humble before God. Tell God everything you are feeling—all you are afraid of and whatever causes you concern. The Bible says that "God resists the proud, but gives grace to the humble" (James 4:6). What you don't need is resistance from God. You need His grace. "Humble yourselves under the mighty hand of God, that He may exalt you in due time, casting all your care upon Him, for He cares for you"

(1 Peter 5:6-7). The best way to humble yourself is in praise and worship and in fasting and prayer.

We can keep reading God's Word and living His way. When difficulty is in your life, don't forget to depend on God and His Word. Ask Him to help you live according to His laws and His ways and do everything according to His will. "My son, do not forget my law, but let your heart keep my commands" (Proverbs 3:1). Make sure that your heart is in alignment with God's Word. You can always find hope reading the Word of God.

We can give praise and worship to God. Praise and worship shakes up the spirit realm and liberates us from discouragement. Praise is one of the ways we encourage ourselves in the Lord. When we praise God, He pours into us His love, peace, joy, and hope, which give us great encouragement.

We can trust that God is good. When bad things happen, you must keep reminding yourself of God's goodness so that you don't ever blame Him for what happens. Seek after Him and wait on Him, and you will see His goodness manifest in your situation. "The LORD is good to those who wait for Him, to the soul who seeks Him" (Lamentations 3:25).

We can encourage and bless other people. It is amazing how it always makes *you* feel better when you make *other people* feel better. Helping others in some way, even if it is only to pray for them, takes your mind off your own concerns. Things change in your own life when you help others.

We can strengthen our faith in God's promises. Faith enables you to overcome whatever life or the adversary throws at you. "Whatever is born of God overcomes the world. And this is the victory that has overcome the world—our faith" (1 John 5:4). Remind yourself every day to believe God's promises to you, so you can hold fast to them.

STANDING ON GOD'S PROMISES

In order to keep from losing hope and giving up, you have to not only *know* God's promises and cling to them in deep faith, but you must also determine that the ground you stand on is supported by those truths. As long as you choose to stand on God's promises and refuse to give up, you will win. In difficult times—when the struggle seems too great, and you're weary and feel like giving up—speak these promises over and over.

Below are just a few of the many promises I am talking about, but I *promise* that when you put your faith in them, they will keep you from losing heart.

A promise if you obey God. "You shall walk in all the ways which the LORD your God has commanded you, that you may live and that it may be well with you, and that you may prolong your days in the land which you shall possess" (Deuteronomy 5:33).

A promise when you seek God's counsel. "Nevertheless I am continually with You; You hold me by my right hand. You will guide me with Your counsel, and afterward receive me to glory" (Psalm 73:23-24).

A promise of protection. "The LORD shall preserve you from all evil; He shall preserve your soul. The LORD shall preserve your going out and your coming in from this time forth, and even forevermore" (Psalm 121:7-8).

A promise that God will hear your prayer. "You will call upon Me and go and pray to Me, and I will listen to you" (Jeremiah 29:12).

A promise when your heart is broken. "The LORD is near to those who have a broken heart, and saves such as have a contrite spirit" (Psalm 34:18).

A promise to deliver you in time of need. "He will deliver the needy when he cries, the poor also, and him who has no helper" (Psalm 72:12).

A promise when you need wisdom. "The LORD gives wisdom; from His mouth come knowledge and understanding; He stores up sound wisdom for the upright; He is a shield to those who walk uprightly" (Proverbs 2:6-7).

A promise of great things ahead. "Eye has not seen, nor ear heard, nor have entered into the heart of man the things which God has prepared for those who love Him" (1 Corinthians 2:9).

A promise in time of trouble. "Though I walk in the midst of trouble, You will revive me; You will stretch out Your hand against the wrath of my enemies, and Your right hand will save me" (Psalm 138:7).

A promise when you feel weak. "He gives power to the weak, and to those who have no might He increases strength" (Isaiah 40:29).

A promise when you need courage. "Be of good courage, and He shall strengthen your heart, all you who hope in the LORD" (Psalm 31:24).

A promise when you feel threatened. "'No weapon formed against you shall prosper, and every tongue which rises against you in judgment You shall condemn. This is the heritage of the servants of the LORD, and their righteousness is from Me,' says the LORD" (Isaiah 54:17).

A promise when you need help. "God is our refuge and strength, a very present help in trouble. Therefore we will not fear, even though the earth be removed, and though the mountains be carried into the midst of the sea" (Psalm 46:1-2).

A promise when you need faith to believe God will answer your prayers. "Whatever things you ask in prayer, believing, you will receive" (Matthew 21:22).

A promise to wait for you. "The LORD will wait, that He may be gracious to you; and therefore He will be exalted, that He may have mercy on you. For the LORD is a God of justice; blessed are all those who wait for Him" (Isaiah 30:18).

God has planned restoration for every part of your life. You not only received new life when you received the Lord, but you have also received the power to grow in that life every day from then on. Because of the Holy Spirit in you, God will continue the work He began in you until you go to be with Him. "Being confident of this very thing, that He who has begun a good work in you will complete it until the day of Jesus Christ" (Philippians 1:6). This restoration process is something you cannot keep from happening if your heart is with God in every day. No matter where you are at the moment, He will continue to restore you to your original intended condition

God will *never* give up on you. So don't you give up on Him. If you keep walking close to God, you will be living a life of freedom, wholeness, and true success—a life that works.

⇾ PRAYER POWER ⇽

Lord, my hope is in You, and I know You will never fail me. Thank You that Your restoration is ongoing in my life. I am grateful that I am Your child and You have given me a purpose. Thank You for the great future You have for me because You love me (1 Corinthians 2:9). Thank You that I am never alone (Matthew 28:20). Thank You that I am complete in You (Colossians 2:10).

Lord, help me to not think of giving up when things become difficult. Keep me from losing patience or courage. Help me to remember that even in hard times You will help me persevere.

Keep me from becoming discouraged in times of waiting. I know Your timing is perfect and the way You do things is right. Help me to cling to Your promises so that they are engraved upon my heart and are alive within me. Enable me to "not remember the former things, nor consider the things of old." I know You are doing a new thing in me. I pray it will "spring forth" speedily. I pray You will "make a road in the wilderness and rivers in the desert" for me (Isaiah 43:18-19).

Lord, I hope for what I do not yet see, for I know that "hope that is seen is not hope" (Romans 8:24). I know I'm in a hurry for things to happen. Forgive me if I have tried to put You on my schedule. I pray that by patience I will possess my soul (Luke 21:19). Thank You that You "will perfect that which concerns me" (Psalm 138:8).

In Jesus' name I pray.

✧ WORD POWER ✧

Therefore we do not lose heart. Even though our outward man is perishing, yet the inward man is being renewed day by day.

2 CORINTHIANS 4:16

"For the mountains shall depart and the hills be removed, but My kindness shall not depart from you, nor shall My covenant of peace be removed," says the LORD, who has mercy on you.

ISAIAH 54:10

Let us not grow weary while doing good, for in due season we shall reap if we do not lose heart.

GALATIANS 6:9

I will bless the LORD who has given me counsel; my heart also instructs me in the night seasons.

I have set the LORD always before me; because
He is at my right hand I shall not be moved.

PSALM 16:7-8

The LORD bless you and keep you; the LORD make His
face shine upon you, and be gracious to you; the LORD
lift up His countenance upon you, and give you peace.

NUMBERS 6:24-26

❖ Personal Notes ❖

✣ PERSONAL NOTES ✣

❖ Personal Notes ❖

✧ Personal Notes ✧

✦ Personal Notes ✦

✦ PERSONAL NOTES ✦

✦ PERSONAL NOTES ✦

✛ Personal Notes ✛

✦ PERSONAL NOTES ✦

✦ Personal Notes ✦

→ Personal Notes ←

✦ PERSONAL NOTES ✦

Lead Me, Holy Spirit

The Holy Spirit wants those who know Him to hear when He speaks to their heart, soul, and spirit. He is there to help believers enter into the relationship with God they yearn for, the wholeness and freedom God has for them, and the fulfillment of God's promises to them.

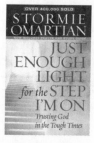

Just Enough Light for the Step I'm On

New Christians and those experiencing life changes or difficult times will appreciate Stormie's honesty, candor, and advice based on experience and the Word of God in this collection of devotional readings perfect for the pressure of today's world.

The Prayer That Changes Everything®

Stormie's warm, personal stories, biblical truths, and practical guiding principles reveal the changes to circumstances that can take place when Christians offer praise during times of difficulty, sorrow, fear, and, yes, abundance and joy.

To learn more about books by Stormie Omartian
or to read sample chapters, log on to our website:

www.harvesthousepublishers.com

HARVEST HOUSE PUBLISHERS
EUGENE, OREGON